P9-CBD-832

Oceans in Motion

This bioluminescent hydromedusa adds light to the ocean.

AUTHORS

Mary Atwater
The University of Georgia

Prentice Baptiste
University of Houston

Lucy Daniel
Rutherford County Schools

Jay Hackett
University of Northern Colorado

Richard Moyer
University of Michigan, Dearborn

Carol Takemoto
Los Angeles Unified School District

Nancy Wilson
Sacramento Unified School District

Macmillan/McGraw-Hill
School Publishing Company
New York   **Columbus**

Environmental Education:
Cheryl Charles, Ph.D.
Executive Director
Project Wild
Boulder, CO

Gifted:
Dr. James A. Curry
Associate Professor, Graduate Faculty
College of Education, University of Southern Maine
Gorham, ME

Global Education:
M. Eugene Gilliom
Professor of Social Studies and Global Education
The Ohio State University
Columbus, OH

Life Science:
Wyatt W. Anderson
Professor of Genetics
University of Georgia
Athens, GA

Orin G. Gelderloos
Professor of Biology and Professor of Environmental Studies
University of Michigan—Dearborn
Dearborn, MI

Donald C. Lisowy
Education Specialist
New York, NY

Dr. E.K. Merrill
Assistant Professor
University of Wisconsin Center—Rock County
Madison, WI

Literature:
Dr. Donna E. Norton
Texas A&M University
College Station, TX

Derrick R. Lavoie
Assistant Professor of Science Education
Montana State University
Bozeman, MT

CONSULTANTS

Assessment:
Mary Hamm
Associate Professor
Department of Elementary Education
San Francisco State University
San Francisco, CA

Cognitive Development:
Pat Guild, Ed.D.
Director, Graduate Programs in Education and Learning Styles Consultant
Antioch University
Seattle, WA

Kathi Hand, M.A.Ed.
Middle School Teacher and Learning Styles Consultant
Assumption School
Seattle, WA

Earth Science:
David G. Futch
Associate Professor of Biology
San Diego State University
San Diego, CA

Dr. Shadia Rifai Habbal
Harvard-Smithsonian Center for Astrophysics
Cambridge, MA

Tom Murphree, Ph.D.
Global Systems Studies
Monterey, CA

Suzanne O'Connell
Assistant Professor
Wesleyan University
Middletown, CT

Sidney E. White
Professor of Geology
The Ohio State University
Columbus, OH

Macmillan/McGraw-Hill School Division
10 Union Square East
New York, New York 10003
Printed in the United States of America

ISBN 0-02-276134-9 / 7

2 3 4 5 6 7 8 9 RRW 99 98 97 96 95

Mathematics:

Dr. Richard Lodholz
Parkway School District
St. Louis, MO

Middle School Specialist:

Daniel Rodriguez
Principal
Pomona, CA

Misconceptions:

Dr. Charles W. Anderson
Michigan State University
East Lansing, MI

Dr. Edward L. Smith
Michigan State University
East Lansing, MI

Multicultural:

Bernard L. Charles
Senior Vice President
Quality Education for Minorities Network
Washington, DC

Paul B. Janeczko
Poet
Hebron, MA

James R. Murphy
Math Teacher
La Guardia High School
New York, NY

Clifford E. Trafzer
Professor and Chair, Ethnic Studies
University of California, Riverside
Riverside, CA

Physical Science:

Gretchen M. Gillis
Geologist
Maxus Exploration Company
Dallas, TX

Henry C. McBay
Professor of Chemistry
Morehouse College and Clark Atlanta University
Atlanta, GA

Wendell H. Potter
Associate Professor of Physics
Department of Physics
University of California, Davis
Davis, CA

Claudia K. Viehland
Educational Consultant, Chemist
Sigma Chemical Company
St. Louis, MO

Reading:

Charles Temple, Ph.D.
Associate Professor of Education
Hobart and William Smith Colleges
Geneva, NY

Safety:

Janice Sutkus
Program Manager: Education
National Safety Council
Chicago, IL

Science Technology and Society (STS):

William C. Kyle, Jr.
Director, School Mathematics and Science Center
Purdue University
West Lafayette, IN

Social Studies:

Jean Craven
District Coordinator of Curriculum Development
Albuquerque Public Schools
Albuquerque, NM

Students Acquiring English:

Mario Ruiz
Pomona, CA

STUDENT ACTIVITY TESTERS

Alveria Henderson
Kate McGlumphy
Katherine Petzinger
John Wirtz
Sarah Wittenbrink

Andrew Duffy
Chris Higgins
Sean Pruitt
Joanna Huber
John Petzinger

FIELD TEST TEACHERS

Kathy Bowles
Landmark Middle School
Jacksonville, FL

Myra Dietz
#46 School
Rochester, NY

John Gridley
H.L. Harshman Junior High School #101
Indianapolis, IN

Annette Porter
Schenk Middle School
Madison, WI

Connie Boone
Fletcher Middle School
Jacksonville, FL

Theresa Smith
Bates Middle School
Annapolis, MD

Debbie Stamler
Sennett Middle School
Madison, WI

Margaret Tierney
Sennett Middle School
Madison, WI

Mel Pfeiffer
I.P.S. #94
Indianapolis, IN

CONTRIBUTING WRITER

Katherine Kenah

ACKNOWLEDGEMENTS

Sea Song by Thomas Lovell Beddoes.

Shark near a coral reef.

Oceans in Motion

Lessons

Themes

Activities!

Features

 Links

Departments

Oceans are home to the fascinating and awesome from one-celled creatures to the massive whale.

Oceans in Motion

How do people know the contents of the oceans? How are their mysteries revealed?

Early explorers feared the real and imagined dangers of the ocean.

The ocean covers more than 70 percent of Earth's surface. It is far more than a place to swim and boat. Food, energy, minerals, and medicines exist there in abundance. Ships use its waters to transport people and goods between continents. The ocean keeps us from frying in some parts of the world and freezing in others. Rain originates in the sea. Without the ocean, Earth would be a barren, lifeless planet.

Early oceanographers faced fearful limitations when confronted with the vastness of the ocean world. They did not have the technology available that today allows scientists to probe the very depths of the sea with miniature equipment and delicate computer-driven instruments and cameras. In fact, the earliest explorers set sail with few maps or incomplete ones bearing dire warnings like "Here Be Dragons" inked in for regions yet unknown.

Step by step, small ideas and new inventions expanded the range of people's explorations of the oceans and increased the importance and usefulness of the sea in their lives. Try the next activity to help you visualize one such invention.

Activity!

A Simple Raft

When early humans watched individual logs floating in the ocean, they saw them roll. By lashing several together, they made the first kind of boat. You can do the same.

What You Need

4 pencils, small pan, water, masking tape, Activity Log page 1

Put a single pencil in a tub full of water and make waves near it by pumping your open hand up and down underwater. Watch the pencil. How many motions do you see? Now, take four pencils and tie them together with masking tape, side by side, so they form a flat surface. Place them in the water and generate more waves. What difference do you see between the single pencil and the small pencil raft? If you were an early explorer, which would you choose for your boat? Record all observations and answers in your **Activity Log**.

Have you ever watched a leaf drifting across a puddle or lake? If it is curled up at the sides, it stays afloat much longer. Early civilizations used this same principle in their explorations of the oceans. They hollowed out logs to be used as boats, in a way similar to the raft you created in the previous activity. They realized they could maneuver their boats over the ceiling of the sea with their paddles. The more paddles and people aboard, the farther they could go.

As the oceans became more familiar, people learned more specialized ways to increase their livelihood or knowledge. Those persons fishing in the ocean learned to cast weighted lines over the sides of boats to take depth soundings. Knowing how deep the water was helped them know how far down they had to lower their fishing nets. But what about the ocean beyond the range of these small boats? What about the ocean realms beyond the reach of those weighted lines?

When Ferdinand Magellan (Fûr'din and' Ma jel'ən) set sail around the world in 1519, it was believed that the deep sea was bottomless. In fact, the floor of the ocean is still called the Abyss, the Greek word for *bottomless*. Magellan's ship carried on board 200 fathoms of rope to sound the depths (a fathom is 6 feet). Between the Coral Islands of Saint Paul and Les Tiburones (Lā Tē bûr on) in the Pacific, his ropes hit nothing, and he logged that spot as the deepest place in the Pacific Ocean. He made an important discovery . . . but not the one he realized. His rope crossed the divide between the continental shelf and the continental slope. The knowledge that the ocean floor was roughly 1,500 meters (5,000 feet) beyond the reach of his rope was still hundreds of years in the future.

The real knowledge of the world beneath the ceiling of the sea began in 1839 with a horse and coach accident! As he was returning to his ship on a horse-drawn coach, a young seaman named Matthew Fontaine Maury was thrown from his seat when the coach overturned in soft mud. His knee was crushed. Sea voyages were out of the question. During his long, slow recovery, Maury gathered together the current knowledge of the sea at that time and published the first map of the ocean floor. In 1854 he published a book about the sea that captured everyone's imagination. Maury's book was the beginning of oceanography, the study of the seas.

Four days before Christmas in 1872, the *H.M.S. Challenger* left port in Britain.

Embarking with several naturalists, wire, rope, and a laboratory filled with thousands of glass bottles for specimens, the *Challenger's* mission was "an exploration of the Deep Sea throughout all the Great Oceanic Basins." For those on board, it really was the equivalent of going to the moon. The big question facing them—Was there life at the bottom of the deep sea beyond the continental shelf?

They set sail and immediately ran into a winter storm in the English Channel. Unlike earlier vessels plying the water, the *Challenger* had an engine along with sails. She could hold steady at a station, while winches lowered dredges and nets over the side, without being blown about by winds.

H.M.S. Challenger's 1872 voyage brought back a wealth of marine knowledge that is still valued today.

Besides rope and wire, the ship also carried a bore, a tube 7.5 centimeters (3 inches) across, to sink into the undersea floor and bring up its contents so the scientists could observe the contents of the seafloor. It took all day to make a single sounding, lowering the bore miles into the water on the end of a rope. The first occurred off the Canary Islands in more than three miles of water. The catch contained no life-forms, only thick, chocolate-colored clay. A second attempt was made . . . and up came worms! The crew of the *H.M.S. Challenger* had their long-awaited answer. There was life at the bottom of the Abyss.

Three-and-a-half years and about 110,000 kilometers (69,000 miles) later, the *Challenger* completed her remarkable voyage with a wealth of knowledge unmatched in the history of marine exploration. The *Challenger's* glass vials contained 4,717 new species of organisms never seen before. The naturalists had succeeded in taking a water depth measurement of approximately 8,000 meters (27,000 feet), the deepest ever recorded. After years of analysis, the findings of the *Challenger* expedition were published in 50 volumes. The findings are still used and valued today.

Like the voyage of the *H.M.S. Challenger*, deep-sea exploration today is still filled with unknowns. It takes hard work and international cooperation to conduct the research that's expanding our knowledge of the oceanic world. Still, we probably know less about the oceans today than we know about the moon! The oceans of the world present an endless frontier for exploration and discovery.

In the following lessons, you will learn about Earth's water cycle and the physical and chemical properties of seawater. You will study the motions of ocean water, and the marine life teeming at every depth. You will examine human interactions and dependence upon the oceans. You will also share in many of the discoveries made by oceanographic explorers, past and present.

Science in Literature

Exploration of the fascinating world of the oceans is still in its infancy. Books can take you on a voyage of the oceans where you can discover more about the rich life of the oceans, study the ecosystems of thousands of plant and animal species, and learn about ocean currents and deep-sea structures that are spectacular beyond belief. Once you understand the beauty and importance of the oceans and how this system interacts with Earth's environment, you can begin to realize your role in helping to preserve this vast natural resource. The following books offer you a magnificent way to explore the mysteries of the oceans.

40364-7 • U.S. $3.25
CAN. $3.95

A DELL YEARLING BOOK

By the three-time Newbery Award Honor Book author

GARY PAULSEN
THE VOYAGE OF THE FROG

The Voyage of the Frog
by Gary Paulsen.
New York: Orchard Books, 1989.

Sailing alone at sea can be a very frightening experience when conditions are turbulent and there is little food on board. In this book, join 14-year-old David as he sails his boat, the 22-foot fiberglass *Frog,* on its last voyage across the Pacific in a raging storm with no radio, no flares, and little food. Travel with David as he encounters screaming winds, towering waves, sharks, and killer whales. This book will grip you to the depths of ultimate excitement as you attempt to help David use strategies to stay alive and maneuver the boat safely home.

Coastal Rescue: Preserving Our Seashores
by Christina G. Miller and Louise A. Berry. New York: Antheneum, 1989.

In this book you will be introduced to the problems, natural and human-made, facing our shores, how people have used the coastlines through centuries, and why today the United States is faced with making important decisions on the use and preservation of our coasts before it's too late. It is hoped that reading this book will make you more aware of these problems and help you focus on steps being taken to save our shores and the ways you can help.

Other Good Books To Read

A Walk on the Great Barrier Reef
by C. Arnold. Minneapolis: Carolrhoda Books, Inc., 1988.

This book leads you on a tour of discovery as you explore the structure of the Great Barrier Reef and the habits of its varied inhabitants.

Keeper of the Light
by Jan O'Donnell Klaveness. New York: Morrow Junior Books, 1990.

Ian, a young boy from Illinois, finds excitement, suspense, and mystery as he explores the coast of the Atlantic Ocean for the first time in search of his grandmother's will.

Protecting the Oceans
by John Baines. Austin, Texas: Steck-Vaughn Library, 1991.

This book focuses on the importance of the many ocean resources, both living and nonliving, and ways we can protect the oceans.

Water can exist as a solid, a liquid, or a gas.

Mist is condensed water vapor.

Earth's Water Cycle

*O*h, water, refreshing water. In this lesson you will investigate the many forms of water and observe its importance as it changes in a complex system called the water cycle.

Minds On! What do you think is the importance of water in your life? You may swim in it, splash friends with it, have snowball fights with it, wash in it, and enjoy the rainbows its droplets paint in the sky. From where does all that water come? Think of the different forms water takes. Think of all the sources of water on Earth. How are they related or interconnected with one another? What differences would exist in your life if you lived in the middle of a dry desert compared to a lush tropical island? How would you adapt to different conditions having varying amounts of precipitation? Record the answers to these questions on page 2 of your *Activity Log.●*

Along with the air we breathe, water is critical to our survival. This is true for every living creature, from the smallest flea to the largest whale. We need water to digest food,

Snow is water in a solid (frozen) state.

eliminate waste, and regulate body temperature. Humans can live without food for nearly a month. Without water, death would occur within a week.

How much water do you drink each day? The average person takes in approximately 60,000 liters (16,000 gallons) of water over the course of a lifetime. When you arrive home thirsty from a jog around the block or the racetrack at school and pour yourself a cold drink, you are pouring billions and billions of water molecules into your glass. Yet every single one of those molecules has been used many times before!

Water isn't only essential to life, it is also a powerful force in its own right. It shapes the world in countless ways. Ice can shatter solid stone, glaciers carve their way through huge mountains, rivers wear away the land to form great valleys, and waves and tides gradually erode and reshape the outlines of coasts the world over.

Only three percent of the water in the world is fresh water. Three-quarters of the world's fresh water is frozen in glaciers, ice caps, and in large masses of floating ice called icebergs. If they suddenly melted, sea level would rise about 60 meters (200 feet) around the world. Vast coastal areas would vanish underwater, including major cities like London, New York, and Tokyo.

Icebergs floating in oceans are hazardous to passing ships. To see why, do the following Try This Activity.

Activity!

Make Your Own Iceberg

You can construct a model of an iceberg.

What You Need

balloon, water, freezer, metric ruler, scissors, deep bucket, plastic bag, *Activity Log* page 3

Fit the balloon over a faucet and fill it with cold water. Knot it tightly to seal the water inside. Put the water-filled balloon inside a plastic bag (without any holes) and place it in a freezer overnight. The next morning, take the balloon out of the freezer and peel away the plastic and rubber. Put your iceberg in a deep bucket of water. Devise a procedure to help you answer these questions— How much of the iceberg is floating above the surface of the water? How much of it is below the water? What have you learned about icebergs that makes them extremely hazardous to passing ships? Record all observations and answer all questions in your ***Activity Log***.

But where did all the water come from? Scientists have offered several hypotheses. The most widely accepted hypothesis begins with the original formation of Earth. As the materials that formed Earth cooled, water was trapped in rocks in Earth's crust. Increasing pressure in Earth's interior along with decay of radioactive materials produced enough thermal energy for Earth's interior to melt. Convection currents set in motion by this thermal energy gradually separated the molten material, with heavier materials sinking and lighter materials rising toward the surface. One substance in these lighter materials was water. Water in the form of water vapor was released into the atmosphere as volcanoes erupted. As the atmosphere cooled, the water vapor condensed and fell to the surface, collecting in the low places in the crust to form Earth's oceans. Water running over Earth's

Sources of Water

Clouds

Oceans

Look at the different sources of water on these two pages. Can you think of other sources of water that exist on Earth?

surface dissolved salts and other substances from the rocks and carried these substances to the oceans, making them salty.

So what exactly is water? In 1781, a British scientist named Joseph Priestly proved that water was made by uniting two gases, hydrogen and oxygen, in the proportion of two atoms of hydrogen to every one of oxygen. He also proved that one drop of water contained billions of molecules made up of hydrogen and oxygen.

In this lesson you will follow water as it moves through different interactions, absorbing and releasing energy, within a continuous cycle. One of the most important processes in this continuous cycle of water is evaporation. Evaporation is the process whereby a liquid is changed to its gaseous state. What are the factors that influence the evaporation of water, and how do they work? Let's explore the next activity to find out.

Hydrogen

Oxygen

Hydrogen

Water molecule

Icebergs

Spring flowing from groundwater

Freshwater lakes and rivers

Activity!

What Factors Affect Evaporation Rate?

You can design and conduct an experiment to determine how certain factors affect the evaporation of water.

What You Need

pan balance
sponges of different sizes
scissors
plastic sandwich bag
spotlight
hot water
cold water
electric fan
jar lid
Activity Log **pages 4–5**

What To Do

1 There are several factors that may affect the rate at which water evaporates. Before looking at the *Activity Log,* list some factors that you (as a group) think might cause water to evaporate faster or slower. Then, using the materials provided, set up an experiment designed to test the effect of one of those factors on the evaporation of water. Next, predict the effect the factor you are testing will have on the rate of evaporation. Record this prediction in your *Activity Log* page 4.

These materials can be used to test the factors that affect evaporation rate.

16 See the *Safety Tip* in step 2.

2 Next, conduct the experiment using the materials provided to test your prediction. Record the steps in your *Activity Log*. *Safety Tip:* If you use the fan, be sure to keep all parts of it dry at all times. (Remember that your experiment must have a control and a variable. Every factor should be exactly the same, except the one factor that you are testing. Also, remember to weigh all sponges before and after being used in an experiment. Sponges must be kept on a smooth, waterproof surface throughout the activity.)

3 Compare your results with other groups testing the same factor.

4 Share your results with other groups who are testing different factors.

What Happened?

In your *Activity Log,* explain how each of the tested factors influenced the rate of evaporation.

What Now?

1. From what you have observed, in which area would you expect the greater evaporation rate? Give reasons to support your choices.
   a. Arctic Ocean or the Gulf of Mexico?
   b. Calm or windy areas of the Mediterranean Sea?
2. Explain how the season of the year affects the rate of evaporation from the oceans.

EXPLORE

How Is Water Recycled?

As you saw in the last Explore Activity, many factors affect water evaporation. Warm temperatures, wind, large surface areas, and the energy of the sun all increase the rate of evaporation. Shade, cool temperatures, high humidity, and small surface areas decrease the rate of evaporation.

Earth obtains small amounts of new water each time a volcano erupts and releases water vapor into the atmosphere. But in general, the water we use today is the same water that has been used for millions of years. Water is a vital resource and must be used over and over again. In this respect, it is reusable. Water moves from place to place in a large, complex system called the **water cycle.** Water is not just contained in the bodies of organisms like you, your friends, your pets, and your plants. Water covers more than 70 percent of Earth's surface. Most of that water is held in the oceans.

Why is evaporation so critical to Earth? Why is it so important to the water cycle? Could it be the generating engine that keeps the world's water cycle turning?

2 These droplets are driven through the atmosphere by wind. The droplets gather into clouds, growing larger and heavier, until they fall from the sky in the form of precipitation, such as rain, hail, or snow. About 75 percent of all precipitation falls back into the ocean. The rest comes down on land.

3 The remaining water drains into rivers and lakes or sinks into the ground. When the ground is saturated by torrential downpours, or when snow melts rapidly, water becomes runoff. Runoff is water that flows across Earth's surface.

4 Water that does not run off seeps into Earth by the process of infiltration (in fil′trā′shən). Eventually this groundwater seeps into creeks and streams that flow into small rivers. Small rivers join larger rivers flowing toward the sea. Slowly the cycle is completed by the evaporation of water back into the atmosphere, only to begin again.

1 Rising water vapor from the oceans contains no salt. As water vapor rises, it cools in the air and changes back to a liquid, or condenses into tiny droplets by the process of *condensation*.

5 Plants absorb about six percent of water from the soil, and release part of it through the surface of their leaves by a process called *transpiration* (tran′ spə rā′ shən).

Only about 25 percent of raindrops from clouds reach land. The rest fall back into the oceans, maintaining the balance between evaporation and condensation, and preventing oceans from becoming even saltier.

How does evaporation take place? What sets off this endless cycle of water motion throughout the world? When you look at a drop of water, it looks calm and still. Yet the molecules in that drop of water are in constant motion invisible to the naked eye.

Because of that motion, every single molecule of water has a tiny amount of thermal energy. Under ordinary conditions, water molecules move very fast. They move faster than the fastest human-made satellites. Increased thermal energy makes the water molecules move even faster. Decreased thermal energy slows their motion. As long as the molecules have enough energy to keep moving and colliding and remain close enough to attract one another electrically, the water will remain liquid.

Have you ever gone roller skating in a crowded roller skating rink? The crowd is in constant motion. Skaters go too fast, lose control, crash into the side walls, keep on skating, or leave the rink altogether. They are behaving similarly to water molecules.

When evaporation occurs the water appears to disappear because of the way its molecules behave. Some collide with each other, ricochet, and zoom off. Some bombard the sides of a container, rebound, and continue moving. But some, in a burst of speed, break loose from the electrical attraction of the other molecules and leave the container altogether. When all the water molecules have entered the air, the liquid water is gone. The water has evaporated completely.

Escaped water molecules form a vapor. This vapor is one of the many gases in air. Like gases in Earth's atmosphere, water vapor is invisible, although it may be observed over a boiling pot as it condenses with the cooler air and becomes a liquid again. Do the Try This Activity on this page to explore the nature of water vapor.

Can you explain the action of water being changed into water vapor in this photograph?

Molecules of water vapor are the same as molecules of liquid water. They have the same weight and size, but they behave differently. Water vapor behaves like other gas molecules. They move freely, traveling faster and farther than liquid molecules.

Properties of Water in the Solid State

Have you ever put a snowball into a freezer and been surprised weeks later to find that it had become smaller? What do you think happened? Let's try the following Try This Activity to find out.

TRY THIS

Activity!

Water Vapor in the Air

You can predict and observe the effect of humidity on the condensation of water vapor from the air.

What You Need
glass jar
ice water
Activity Log **page 6**

Suppose you were to fill a glass with ice water and observe it for several minutes. Predict what will happen. Think about how the humidity or amount of water vapor in the air will affect what happens. Revise your prediction if necessary. Now, try it and see. Record your observations in your *Activity Log*. Explain what caused any changes you observed.

Activity!

From Ice to Vapor

You can observe how a solid changes to a gas without becoming a liquid.

What You Need

small cloth, water, freezer, *Activity Log* page 7

Soak a piece of cloth in water, wring it out, and put it in the freezer. In your *Activity Log,* predict what you think will happen. Observe the cloth after several minutes. Leave the cloth in the freezer for a week and then observe any changes. What do you think happened? Record all observations and explanations in your *Activity Log.*

Many people don't realize that ice can change directly into water vapor. In a process called **sublimation** (sub′ lə mā′ shən), a solid changes to a gas or a gas changes to a solid without becoming a liquid. This is what happened in the above activity. Can you think of other examples of sublimation?

Ice has a solid crystal shape, resulting from the behavior of molecules when water freezes. When the temperature drops, water molecules lose energy to the surroundings and move about more slowly. At freezing temperatures, they slow down so much that the attraction between the molecules is able to hold them together. The water molecules cluster together in a fixed pattern. They vibrate back and forth in a kind of shivering motion, but they do not move from place to place.

If you hold 18 toothpicks and 12 raisins together in a lump, they will take up a certain amount of space. But if you arrange those same toothpicks and raisins into a crystal (a raisin at each connecting point of the toothpicks), the crystal occupies more space than the original lump. Water molecules in ice act in a similar way. Because the molecules are

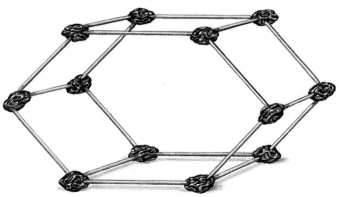

A crystal of ice takes up more space than an equal quantity of water, just as a "crystal" of raisins and toothpicks takes up more space than the raisins and toothpicks combined in a lump.

held fast with spaces between or around them, unable to move about freely, ice takes up more space than water. Water expands when it freezes. Because it expands, solid water, or ice, is less dense and floats on liquid water.

In fact, water has a property that is different from most other liquids, in that most liquids contract and become more dense when they become solids. Water contracts like other liquids when it begins to cool, but as it approaches freezing temperatures it reverses the process as described above. It begins to expand and becomes less dense.

Because of this property, ice that forms in the winter can float on the surface of any body of water. It stays exposed to the sun and melts easily. Imagine what would happen if ice were more dense than water. It would sink to the bottom of lakes, rivers, and oceans. This would happen over and over again. The sun would not reach the ice to melt it. Each year more and more ice would form, until some rivers, lakes, and seas would become solid ice during the winter. There could even be ice at the bottom during summer.

Imagine life in a world with water frozen solid! The great ocean currents, like the Gulf Stream, would cease to flow. They couldn't carry their warming waters toward the Poles. The tropics would become unbearably hot. Temperate zones would grow colder and colder. The impact on life and productivity in the oceans would be devastating worldwide.

Large bodies of water slowly absorb and store thermal energy from the sun during the summer. In winter, this stored thermal energy is released into the atmosphere. In the summer, as water evaporates, it absorbs thermal energy from the air and cools the atmosphere. This interaction is a delicately balanced process that is vital to life on Earth. In this way oceans play a major role in the water cycle. The ocean's great size and the slow rate at which water absorbs and radiates energy have a steadying influence on temperatures in the atmosphere. Try the next activity to observe the importance of the water cycle in a different type of environment.

Particle motion

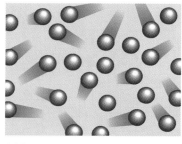

gas

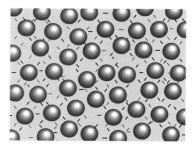

liquid

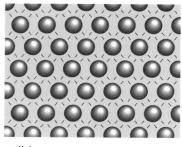

solid

Activity!

Make a Terrarium

You can develop a model of a closed environment in which stages of the water cycle can be observed.

What You Need

2-L plastic soft drink bottle, potting soil, small plants, water, scissors, plastic wrap, masking tape, *Activity Log* page 8

Cut the top off the 2-L bottle using scissors. Then, cover the bottom of the bottle with soil, plant the small plants, and water them. Finally, cover the terrarium with a piece of plastic wrap and seal it.

Observe the terrarium carefully, noting the path of the water through the water cycle. Make a drawing of the terrarium in your *Activity Log*. Use arrows and labels to show where evaporation, condensation, infiltration, and transpiration take place in the terrarium. How does the water cycle in the terrarium compare to the water cycle in an open environment?

Math Link

How Much Water?

S tudy the data in this chart showing the percentages of Earth's water found in the oceans, surface water, ice, and the atmosphere. In your *Activity Log* on page 9, prepare a presentation in graphic form. Also, use the data to construct a physical model illustrating the relative amounts. For example, begin with a liter of water representing the total amount of water on Earth. Calculate, measure, and display the appropriate amounts of water found in the oceans, surface water, ice, and so on. Label and display the relative amounts and percentages in your classroom.

Oceans and sea	97.2%
Ice caps and glaciers	2.15%
Groundwater	0.625%
Lakes and rivers	0.0091%
Atmosphere	0.001%

Interactions With the Water Cycle

Now that you understand the process of how water is changed as it goes through the water cycle, let's look at ways both humans and nature interact with the water cycle. One way is in the production of geothermal power. Geothermal power is generated wherever water comes into contact with hot rocks below Earth's surface. The rocks give off heat that can turn the water into steam. Power companies can drill wells to release the hot water or steam so it can be used to generate energy. The production of geothermal energy can occur only in areas where hot rocks lie near Earth's surface. Iceland, Italy, Japan, the Philippines, New Zealand, and the United States have developed geothermal power plants.

Water power provides 75 percent of New Zealand's electricity. The underground steam in the volcanic area of the North Island of New Zealand is becoming an increasingly important source of power. Near Wairakei (Wī ra′kē), engineers have drilled many deep holes to release geothermal steam. The rising steam is pressurized and super-heated to power machinery, which then generates electricity.

But how does this happen? What is it about Earth's structure that contributes to this process? Is this method of generating electricity always beneficial to those living in the area?

Earth's ground is in many ways like a giant sponge. It is filled with small gaps or spaces called pores. The connections between these spaces allow water to flow through rock and soil. Below the ground surface, these pores are usually filled with a mixture of air and water. Deeper down, these pores are entirely filled with water. It is the upper surface of these water-filled pores that forms the water table.

When power companies drill wells to pump hot water or steam to the surface, the water table immediately under the well is lowered. What happens is similar to when you take a drink with a straw. The water level in your glass is lowered. The local lowering of the water table creates a driving force that causes water to flow toward the well, replacing the water removed by the pumping. This can create devastating problems for the residents of saltwater islands.

Rainfall infiltrating the ground is the source of fresh water for these islands. The rainwater seeps into the pore spaces and raises the level of the water table. The less dense fresh water floats on top of the seawater. If too much fresh water is pumped from wells,

A geothermal power plant

The Greenland ice sheet is one of the world's largest glaciers.

seawater is drawn in, filling the pore spaces emptied of fresh water. Groundwater then becomes contaminated and the island's wells can no longer be used for drinking.

We have discussed the effects of geothermal power as a part of the water cycle. What about other aspects of the cycle? As a part of the water cycle, what are the effects of glaciers on the structure of Earth in certain areas?

Imagine rolling a snowball across your yard, your neighbor's, down the street, and across the school playground . . . and then having it never warm up enough to melt! A large body of moving ice is called a glacier. Exactly when it begins to move depends on how thick it is, the steepness of the surface beneath it, and the surrounding air temperature. Under the pull of gravity, the ice slowly changes shape and moves. Glaciers may advance only 2 to 5 centimeters (1 to 2 inches) in a day or recede in years of warming weather.

Ice sheets are the world's largest glaciers. They exist where more snow falls each winter than melts away during summer. The thick ice flows over large land areas covering everything but the highest mountain peaks.

Ice sheets exist in Greenland and Antarctica. They account for about 95 percent of the world's glacial ice. Greenland is mostly covered by one sheet of ice that is more than 1.6 kilometers (1 mile) deep in spots!

Ice sheets are so heavy they actually cause the underlying rock to sink into Earth. Earth's surface beneath the ice sheets has been pushed hundreds of feet below sea level. After the ice melts, Earth's surface will rise again, like a spongy cake, but it may take many thousands of years. In North America, the land north of the Great Lakes and parts of New England have been rising since the melting away of an ice sheet more than 10,000 years ago!

What does this mean? Consider building a house of cards. You stack them up in delicate rows, thin walls finely balanced. Finally, you have a high tower! Then the cat brushes by and your house of cards comes tumbling down. Like a house of cards, the spongy rebounding of the soil in Alaska has created ground that is very unstable. This ground is called quickclay. It will turn to liquid with a slight vibration and begin to flow downhill!

When the ground was pushed down under the weight of ice sheets, salty mud from seawater settled over the area. The salt made the clay-like mud clump together like a house of cards, with lots of open pore spaces. As the ground rises, fresh rainwater washes the salt from the soil. The bonds between the clumps of clay weaken. A vibration can make the quickclay collapse like a house of cards, and then it flows away because of its high water content.

When ice sheets meet the sea, sometimes huge chunks break off and begin to drift in the water as icebergs. As the icebergs gradually melt, bits of rock, caught up and frozen into the ice, break free and settle to the ocean floor. The trail of rocks across the ocean floor can help scientists understand how ocean currents move.

These rocks were gouged from the action of a moving glacier.

While their majesty and beauty is unquestionable, icebergs, portions of ice sheets, create hazards for ocean vessels.

Some icebergs rise 122 meters (400 feet) above the ocean, but the part of the iceberg beneath the water's surface may reach a depth of 853 meters (2,800 feet)—more than two times the height of the Empire State Building!

381m

122m

762m

853m

King Kong would have to carry Fay Wray two Empire State Buildings higher to reach the total height of this iceberg.

Sum It Up

As you have seen, water on Earth moves from place to place and interacts with the environment in a large, complex system called the water cycle. You discovered that water is a precious resource that moves through a continuous cycle where water is changed and used and reused over and over again. Water has a dramatic impact on Earth's climatic stability and the formation of polar ice sheets. Hopefully you have considered the importance of water in your daily life, and will begin to investigate ways you can contribute to the conservation of this valuable resource.

Using Vocabulary

condensation
infiltration
precipitation
runoff
sublimation
transpiration
water cycle

Using the vocabulary words presented in this lesson, explain the water cycle making sure that someone who has never heard about the water cycle could understand what you have written.

Critical Thinking

1. Draw and label a diagram representing Earth's water cycle and each of its interacting processes.

2. Pretend you are a single water molecule in a glass of water. Using the three states of water, explain how you got there and what happened to you and your fellow water molecules along the way as you traveled through the water cycle. You may want to include water in all three states.

3. Earth's water is called a reusable resource. What does that mean?

4. Describe what might happen along coastal areas if water is pumped from underground wells faster than rainfall can replace it.

5. Identify and explain three different ways people interact with Earth's water cycle.

A freshwater mountain stream has its own special properties.

Ocean water has properties that are different from those of fresh water.

Physical and Chemical Properties of Ocean Water

Who dares to adventure into the depths of the oceans? Those who do will discover how various living and nonliving systems interact in this vast environment due to the specific properties of ocean water.

Look at the photograph of the surfer. Notice the wave the surfer is riding. Are all ocean waves like this one? Suppose he accidently swallows a mouthful of water. How would it taste compared to water from an inland lake? Ocean water and fresh water have many similar properties and some very important differences.

Minds On! Look carefully at the photographs of the surfer and the mountain stream. Imagine you are conducting an experiment for a science fair project. You will analyze water found in these two contrasting environments. You hike up the mountain and fill a bucket with water from a trickling flow in that stream. Then you travel a distance, wade into the ocean with your bucket, and catch the water of a receding wave. When you analyze the contents of your two buckets, what differences do you think you will find? What factors in the environment, living and nonliving, might interact with the water to affect its properties? Use your imagination. Think of everything that could possibly be in the water from those two very different locations. Then list your ideas in your *Activity Log* on page 10.●

If you took a sampling cup no bigger than a cubic inch and headed off into the ocean — able to transport yourself to any region of the world and up and down to any oceanic depth — you would find it difficult to obtain two samples exactly the same . . . anywhere!

Ocean water brims with life-forms (which can be smaller than the period at the end of this sentence or larger than a school bus) and holds a wealth of dissolved minerals and materials. Ocean water evaporates, rises as vapor, and falls to land as rain. When that water completes its cycle and returns to the sea, it carries with it tons of soil and sediment eroded from the land.

In a 24-hour period, the Mississippi River carries 1.8 million metric tonnes (2 million tons) of sediment past the bustling city of New Orleans and on into the Gulf of Mexico. Each year the rivers of the world combined carry 18 billion metric tonnes (20 billion tons) of land to the oceans! This amount of material is just a fraction of what already exists in the waters of the oceans.

In this lesson you will study the chemical and physical properties of ocean water and explore the varied features of the ocean bottom. Let us begin studying these properties by doing the next Explore Activity.

Activity!

Salt Water/Fresh Water

You can explore a property of water that influences how objects float.

What You Need

tall narrow jar
pencil with eraser
salt
spoon
metric ruler
3 L fresh water
3 L salt water
3 L hot water
3 L hot salt water
3 L cold water
3 L cold salt water
thumbtack
waterproof felt-tip pen
paper towels
Activity Log pages 11–12

What To Do

1 Fill a jar with fresh water to within 1 cm of the top.

2 Push the thumbtack into the center of the pencil eraser.

Place the pencil, eraser down, into the water. Then, allow the pencil to float up naturally. Use the waterproof felt-tip pen to mark the pencil at the water line, indicating the pencil's level in the water. *Safety Tip:* Always be careful with sharp objects.

Safety!

See the *Safety Tip* in step 2.

3 Remove the pencil and dry it with a paper towel. Measure the length of the pencil above the water level mark in millimeters and record the length in your *Activity Log*.

4 Repeat steps 1–3 using salt water.

5 Repeat steps 1–3 using both hot and cold salt water and hot and cold fresh water (ice may be used to cool).

What Happened?

1. In which type of water did the pencil float higher? Fresh water or salt water? Hot or cold salt water? Hot or cold fresh water?
2. Predict how the pencil will float if you add several spoonfuls of salt to each type of water previously tested. Try it and record your results in your *Activity Log*.
3. What do you think caused these results?
4. How does the temperature of the water affect floating objects?

What Now?

1. Why is it easier to swim in the ocean than in fresh water?
2. Can a boat carry a heavier load in fresh water or salt water? Why?

EXPLORE

33

Salinity of Ocean Water

Ocean water is very different from the water you drink. Ocean water is salty. It contains many different kinds of dissolved minerals or salts. The amount of dissolved salts in the ocean is referred to as its **salinity** (sə lin′i tē). The greater the percentage of dissolved salts, the higher the salinity of ocean water. The average salinity of ocean water is about 35 grams of dissolved salt per 1,000 grams of water.

The salt dissolved in the ocean was once a part of rocks on land. Rivers eroded the rocks and carried bits of salt and other minerals into the ocean. This action resulted in the accumulation of salt in the seas for millions of years. It has been estimated that there are about 45 quadrillion metric tonnes (50 quadrillion tons) of salt in the oceans of the world.

In the previous Explore Activity, you observed that salinity affects the density of water. The more salt there is dissolved in the water, the more dense the water becomes. Water exerts an upward push on any object dropped into it. This upward pressure is called its upward buoyant (boi′ ənt) force. As water becomes saltier and more dense, its upward buoyant force increases. It pushes up with more strength against the objects floating in it. That is why the pencil floats higher in the jar with salt water. The more dissolved salt, or the higher the salinity, the higher the pencil floats. Do the next Try This Activity to help you increase your understanding of properties of ocean water.

TRY THIS Activity!

Diving Raisins

You can use raisins to help you explore an important property of ocean water.

What You Need

seltzer water, 5 raisins, transparent plastic jar, *Activity Log* page 13

Hypothesize what you think will happen if you drop 4 or 5 raisins, one at a time, into a glass of bubbly seltzer water. Write your hypothesis in your *Activity Log*. Try it, wait for a moment, and then observe what happens. Record your observations in your *Activity Log*. The raisins' wild ride demonstrates an important property of ocean water. What is this property? In your *Activity Log*, record what you think caused the raisins to react this way. This property is utilized by plants, animals, and humans on and in oceans everywhere. It's vital to their safety and survival. You will learn more about this property later in this lesson.

glass again. Then more bubbles cling to their sides and the raisins repeat their ascent!

The raisins sink because their density is greater than the density of the water. The gas bubbles in the seltzer water act like tiny balloons clinging to the sides of the raisins, decreasing their density enough to float to the top of the glass. When the raisins lose the bubbles at the surface, their density becomes greater than the density of the water once again and they fall.

Submersibles use a change in density to raise or lower the craft.

Buoyancy affects a scuba diver's ability to rise when submerged.

The ability to regulate **buoyancy** (boi′ ən sē), or the ability to rise when submerged, is critical to the safety of surfers, swimmers, deep-sea divers, submarines, and countless forms of marine life. In the raisin activity, you saw that when raisins sink to the bottom of a glass of seltzer water, bubbles begin to cling to their sides. The raisins rise upward through the seltzer water. When they reach the surface, the bubbles pop or break away, and the raisins spin over and sink to the bottom of the

The mini-submarines, or submersibles, used by oceanographers rise and sink in much the same way—by changing their density. These research vessels dive by gradually filling flotation tanks inside their hulls with water. After completing their dive and explorations, they pump the water out of these tanks. This reduces the density of the sub, and it rises to the surface. Marine treasure hunters use this simple principle of buoyancy to recover valuable treasures.

In some areas of ocean water, where the evaporation rate is high and annual precipitation is low, the salinity is higher than average. The rapid rate of evaporation increases the salt concentration in the water left behind. The problem is further complicated because of the lack of rainfall to dilute the salty water.

In other areas rainfall outpaces evaporation. Fresh water is pouring into the oceans faster than water is being lost by evaporation. As a result, these areas of the ocean have a lower-than-average salinity. What would you predict about the salinity of ocean water at the mouth of major rivers like the Amazon? Why?

About 3.5 percent of the sea is salt. Some bodies of water are saltier than others. The degree of salinity depends to a large extent on the climate of a region. The Mediterranean Sea, for instance, is relatively salty. It's in a hot, dry climate. The hot air causes rapid surface water evaporation. This leaves a high concentration of salt behind. Since most of the Mediterranean is cut off from other bodies of water by land, little water flows in to dilute the salt.

The relative proportions of dissolved materials are shown in the graph on this page. Although there are many different kinds of materials dissolved in the ocean, the most abundant material is the same as plain table salt—sodium and chlorine. In fact, the salt you use at home (sodium chloride) was once dissolved in an ocean.

Scientists have hypothesized that there are two main sources of salts for ocean water. Some products of chemical weathering of minerals and rocks are soluble in water moving through soil. These dissolved salts make their way into rivers and then into the oceans. Sodium chloride (table salt) is the most abundant salt dissolved in ocean water. Certain elements, such as chlorine, bromine, and sulfur, are more abundant in ocean water than in rocks in Earth's crust. They are more common in gases and water erupted from active volcanoes. This has led many scientists to believe that dissolved gases from volcanoes contribute significantly to the salinity of oceans.

Although weathering, erosion, and volcanic activity continue through time, the salinity of oceans doesn't appear to be increasing. In fact, the salinity of the ocean may change by only one percent in 6 million years. It would appear that salts are being removed as rapidly as they are being added. Some salts are taken from ocean water by plants and animals to build their shells and skeletons. Others are chemically precipitated from ocean water as sediments on the seafloor.

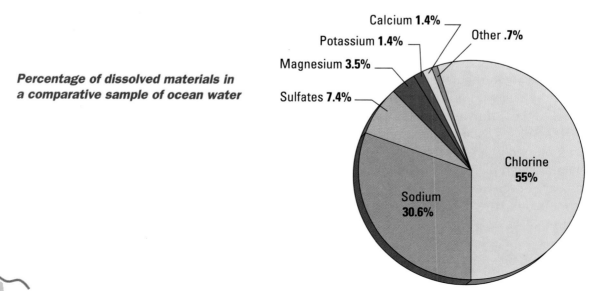

Percentage of dissolved materials in a comparative sample of ocean water

Calcium **1.4%**

Potassium **1.4%**

Magnesium **3.5%**

Sulfates **7.4%**

Other **.7%**

Chlorine **55%**

Sodium **30.6%**

Components of the Oceans

Much of the sediment that covers the seafloor is comprised of the shells of tiny marine animals that have died and drifted to the bottom of the ocean. Oceanographic ships take vertical samples — called cores — of this sediment. Core samples of sediment look like wide lengths of brown toothpaste when stretched across a table. When a small bit of mud from a core is washed through a sieve, the mud vanishes down the drain and a tiny white cluster of microscopic shells remains. These are the shells of foraminifera (fər am′ə nif′ ə rä), tiny marine organisims with calcium-carbonate shells.

It may take millions of years for a thick layer of sediment to accumulate on the seafloor. A core sample from an area where sediment accumulates slowly can hold the history of 600,000 years in its length of mud! Oceanographers have discovered that some of the tiny animals whose shells remain in the sediment were temperature-sensitive. Their shells coiled in different directions in warm than in

Microscopic foraminifera shells like the ones shown above are found in core samples.

Sediment cores are taken by piston corers, consisting mainly of a metal tube of an internal piston. When the corer hits the ocean floor, the piston stops, but the tube goes on into the sediment, enclosing a sample that is held by clasps at the tips of the tube.

cold waters. If the shells coiled to the right in one section of the core, but the shells in the next section coiled to the left, that change marked a shift in the world's climate at the time those animals were alive, and at the place where the core was taken.

By examining the patterns of left and right coiling in the shells down the length of a core, scientists can make a climatic map dating back hundreds of thousands of years! They can determine when ice sheets might have come and gone or when great warming global currents shifted. Can you begin to see how the life within the ocean may reflect changes in climate?

Of the 109 known elements, at least 80 have been found dissolved in the ocean! Gold and silver are two of these elements. In 1927–28, in an attempt to try to pay off debts incurred during World War I, a German chemist, Fritz Haber, equipped an oceanographic ship, the *Meteor,* to rake the waters of the Atlantic. Haber hoped by doing so to recover some of the gold dissolved in seawater. One cubic kilometer of seawater (1,000 billion liters) contains six kilograms of gold. In the vast oceans of the world, it has been estimated that there may be 9 million tonnes (10 million tons) of dissolved gold! In one cubic mile of ocean water, there are about 11 to 14 kilograms (25 to 30 pounds) of gold and about 900 kilograms (2,000 pounds) of silver. Haber abandoned his efforts, however. It was too expensive and difficult to recover even tiny amounts of the precious metals.

Air is also dissolved in ocean water. Oxygen and carbon dioxide are two gases important to life in the ocean as well as life on land. Both of these gases are dissolved in ocean water. These dissolved gases allow fish and plants to live in the ocean. In places where pollution or other conditions have taken these gases from the ocean, there is no plant or animal life.

The temperature of ocean water varies around the world. Close to the equator, the midday sun is high overhead. The more vertical the sun's rays, the more energy is absorbed in a given area. Thus, the surface ocean water near the equator is as warm as 28°C (82°F). Near the poles, the midday sun angle is very low. The lower the sun's angle, the less energy is absorbed in a given area. The surface water at the North and South Poles may be as cold as −1°C (30°F). At both poles, the deeper water is about the same temperature as the surface water. But in most of the ocean, deeper water is colder. The water at the bottom of the oceans is colder than −1°C (30°F). Performing the next Try This Activity can help you understand how ocean temperatures compare to those on land.

Sun's rays

The temperatures of the world's oceans vary depending on the angle at which the sun's rays strike Earth.

Earth

This illustration is not to scale.

Activity!

Energy of the Ocean

You can compare how continents and oceans absorb energy from the sun.

What You Need

2 coffee cans, 2 thermometers, soil, water, stopwatch, *Activity Log* page 14

Fill one coffee can 2/3 full of water and the other to the same level with dry soil. Set up one thermometer so that its bulb is about 1 cm under the surface of the soil and another 1 cm beneath the surface of the water. Place both containers in direct sunlight. Record temperatures on each of the thermometers every 2 min for 10 min. Move them both to the shade and continue recording temperatures each min for 10 more min. Which heats faster, water or land? Which cools faster? Now, predict which heats and cools more quickly—the air above the soil or the air above the water. How could you design an experiment to test your hypothesis? Record all observations and answers in your ***Activity Log***.

What does the above activity tell you about land and ocean climates? Because water heats and cools more slowly than land, climates near the ocean are generally cooler in the summer and warmer in the winter than inland climates. On hot summer days, the land is quickly heated while the ocean remains cooler. Cool air above the ocean blows onto the land and helps lower the hot afternoon temperatures. Early in the morning just before daylight, the land may cool down so much that it is actually cooler than the ocean. Once the land becomes cool, this causes the flow of air to change, blowing from the land out over the ocean.

Now that you have some idea of the ocean surface and how it interacts with the environment, let's expand our depth and see what we can observe about the deeper part of the ocean.

Sun

Features of the Ocean Floor

*I*f you were asked to describe Earth's features, you could probably describe mountains, plains, rivers, forests, and many other features that are visible from Earth's surface. You could probably also describe the surface of the ocean as well as other bodies of water. But what about the ocean floor? What would it look like if all water were drained from the ocean? It might surprise you to know that features of the ocean floor are similar to those of Earth's surface. Oceanographers have studied the ocean floor and found that it is characterized by a great diversity of features. The illustration on this page represents some features of the ocean as they would be seen if all water in the ocean were removed.

The **continental shelf** is the outermost edge of a continent. It is a gently sloping underwater plain, with an average depth of 183 meters (600 feet) of water. In some places the continental shelf is only a few hundred feet wide. In other parts of the world, it extends for miles. Sunlight penetrates and warms the waters here, and the region is rich with nutrients and marine life.

The **continental slope** is the outer edge of the continental shelf. It drops more sharply toward the seafloor than the shelf, like a steeply slanted wall that averages 3,600 meters (12,000) feet in height!

The **abyssal** (ə bis'əl) **plain** is the flat bottom of the ocean. It is covered with a layer of mud, sand, and remains of organisms that have drifted down from above for millions of years.

Mid-ocean ridges are continuous chains of mountains that run down the center of every major ocean. They wrap around Earth for about 60,000 kilometers (37,000 miles), representing more than 20 percent of Earth's surface.

Deep-ocean **trenches** are long, narrow depressions representing where one plate is descending or being subducted under another. Trenches are the deepest parts of the ocean.

Volcanic activity is associated with trench regions of the ocean floor. The molten rock that leads to volcanic activity of the ocean floor occurs as a result of the melting of a descending plate.

Along the center of some mid-ocean ridges is a deep valley called the **rift valley**. Molten rock pushes up from the center of this rift, spreading the seafloor and pushing the continents apart.

In the summer of 1974, three small submersibles made 47 dives down to the rift valley near the Azores. Equipped with dredges and searchlights, the ships were floating recorders. The geologists on board brought back samples of "new" rocks. They took photos of lava flows coming up from within the rift and being shaped by the surrounding cold water into pillows and elephant trunks and long coils. They saw strange flowers and animals. For the first time, people were seeing Earth being born by observing the formation of rock from the eruption of an underwater volcano. However, the ability to see was limited. One of the scientists said it was like exploring the Grand Canyon in a snowstorm with a flashlight.

How do we know anything about the ocean floor? In spite of our inability to adequately see the ocean floor at great depths, there are excellent maps of the ocean floor showing the locations for a wide variety of features. These maps were taken from depth information of sonar soundings from ships. **Sonar** is an instrument that uses sound waves to locate objects underwater. To see how sonar works, do the following activity.

Activity!

Sonar Mapping

You can develop a model that shows how sonar echoes are used to map the ocean floor.

What You Need

clay, shoe box with lid, pencil, 10 plastic straws, metric ruler, *Activity Log* page 15

Use clay to make an ocean floor landscape on the bottom of a shoe box. Make a steep slope, a flat plain, and another steep slope. The slope must simulate an ocean valley. Mark a straight line down the middle of the box top running from end to end. Use your pencil to poke ten evenly spaced holes in the lid along the line. Number the holes 1–10.

Place the lid on the box. Exchange your box with another group. Insert a plastic straw into each hole in order. Measure how deep each straw goes into the box before it touches bottom. Record the depth for each hole on the data chart in your ***Activity Log***. Use the data to make a graph comparing depth in centimeters to each hole location. Connect the points on the graph. (Make the points on your graph in a downward direction so your points will match the

Data and Observations

Top of the box (sea level)

terrain of your sea-floor box. Otherwise your graph will give you an upside-down image of the clay terrain.) You have just made a profile of the bottom of the box. Which areas would you compare to the ocean floor features studied earlier—continental shelf, continental slope, abyssal plain, rift valley, trenches? Record all observations, illustrations, and answers in your ***Activity Log***.

In your model from the Try This Activity, the straw is used like sonar or sound waves by scientists to determine the depth of the ocean. The time between sending the sonar wave and its return after bouncing off the bottom tells scientists how deep the ocean is at that spot. A series of depths is used to plot the topography of the ocean bottom.

Ocean Technology and Sound

Many discoveries of the oceans have been made due to improved technological advances involving the use of radar. These advances are continuing to make us more knowledgeable about the oceans.

In this day and age when we have mapped the far side of the moon, less than one-tenth of one percent of the ocean floor has ever been seen by human eyes. To investigate all this geologic activity, oceanographers must "see" with sound. The technique is called echo sounding. Sonar equipment transmits a pulse of sound that bounces off an object and returns to the ship. If you know how fast sound travels in water, you can calculate the distance the sound and its echo have traveled and divide by two. Maps showing the depth of an area on the seafloor are called bathymetric (bath′ə met′rik) maps. Using sonar readings from different areas of the ocean floor can give a picture of the land beneath the ocean. The bathymeteric map shown below shows the major landforms of the world's ocean floor. You will notice that features of the ocean floor are much like those on land—huge mountain ranges, long, narrow valleys, and broad basins and plains.

The problem with sending just one beam of sound at a time is that it doesn't give you a lot of detail. The sound bounces off the first thing it hits (the thing closest to the ship in a straight line from the source of the sound). If a sonar pulse is beamed toward an area that includes the top of an underwater mountain and a deep trench, the sound will bounce back from the tallest feature. You will "see" the mountain, but miss the trench. The solution to this problem is to send out several beams of sound at once, allowing oceanographers to receive many readings from the same area.

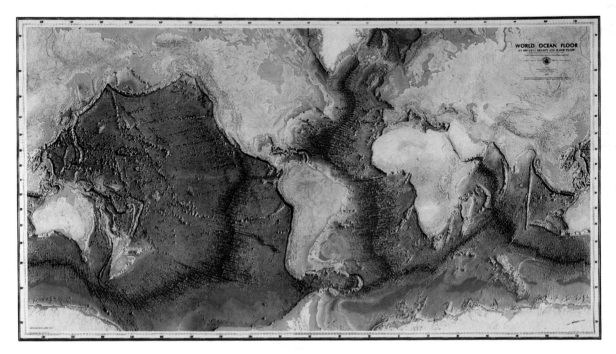

Bathymetric maps show the major landforms of the world's ocean floor.

Math ⏀ Link
Using Sonar

*T*he speed of a sonar wave traveling in ocean water is 1,454 meters (4,798 feet) per second. Suppose that a sonar wave takes eight seconds to reach the bottom and return. How deep is the water at that location?

Focus on Technology

New Ways of Exploring the Ocean Floor

*S*eaBeam is a multi-beam sonar system. It sends out 16 beams in a fanlike pattern from transmitters attached to a ship's hull. It receives back 16 separate echoes from a swath of ocean a mile wide. *SeaBeam* maps are far more detailed than the older, single-beam sonar used for so many years.

To "see" all the nooks and crannies of the ocean, you have to travel well below the surface of the water and as close to the seafloor as possible. Sound spreads as it travels. When you send a beam from the surface, it spreads out so that the area of the ocean floor covered is quite large. Think of a flashlight beam. The farther you hold it from an object, the wider the beam and the fainter the light.

Submersible systems, like the *Jason,* have been invented to travel right down to the seafloor. *Jason* is equipped with both sonar and cameras, but its range is limited. This remote-

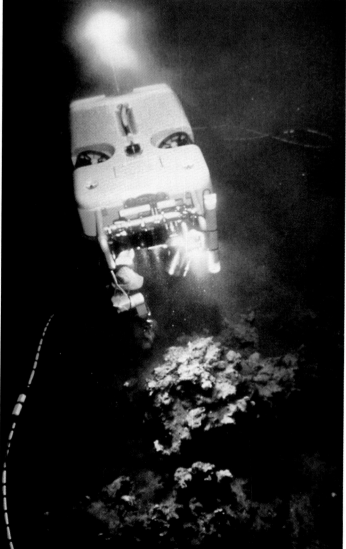

Jason, *an automated submersible, explored the sunken remains of the* **Titanic,** *sending back detailed information.*

operated vehicle explored the sunken remains of the *Titanic* in 1986. It can make maps so detailed that they show the location of worm burrows in the sediment!

There seem to be two options for marine exploration using technology we have today. With *SeaBeam,* scientists can cover a lot of ground and learn less-detailed information, or with *Jason* they can cover a small amount of ground and get detailed descriptions.

Sum It Up

In this lesson you learned that ocean water has measurable physical and chemical properties that vary with movement and depth. The interaction of these properties, such as the impact of salinity on the buoyancy of seawater, was investigated. The actions of various systems within the oceans contribute to global variations, affecting climates on Earth over an extended period of time. Having created a model of your own sea-floor terrain, perhaps you can now visualize the vastness and depth of the ocean. With ocean technology expanding at such a rapid pace, perhaps one day soon exploration of ocean life will be much different than it is today.

Using Vocabulary

abyssal plain   **continental slope**   **salinity**
buoyancy   **mid-ocean ridges**   **sonar**
continental shelf   **rift valley**   **trenches**

Who dares to adventure into the depths of the oceans? You do! You are a science fiction writer who has decided to write about the ocean and the mysteries there. Using what you have learned in the preceding lessons, write a short story using the vocabulary words from this lesson. Have another classmate read it to make sure it makes sense. Be sure to check for proper usage of vocabulary words, spelling, and punctuation. You could illustrate your story if you have time.

Critical Thinking

1. Suppose that a large area of the Gulf of Mexico received much more rainfall than normal over a period of years. Describe how this might affect the salinity of the Gulf water.

2. Consider ocean water in an area where there is high evaporation and low precipitation, such as the Mediterranean Sea. (a) How would its water density compare to ocean water from an area where rainfall is plentiful and temperatures are much lower? (b) Suppose you had samples of both. How could you compare their densities to check your answer?

3. Each year more dissolved minerals are washed from the land into the oceans. Yet, scientists hypothesize that the salinity in the oceans changes little over time. How can you explain this?

4. Why does Seattle, Washington, have such mild winters and moderately cool summers?

5. Draw and label a cross section of the ocean floor showing the continental shelf, continental slope, abyssal plain, mid-ocean ridge, and an ocean-floor trench.

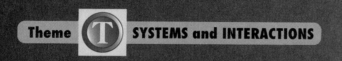

The motion of ocean water is in part responsible for the back-and-forth movement of this ship.

Ocean Water in Motion

C an you describe the motion of ocean water caused by the interaction of waves, currents, and tides?

To Sea! to sea! the calm is o'er
The wanton water leaps in sport,
And rattles down the pebbly shore,
The dolphin wheels, the sea cows snort,
And unseen mermaid's pearly song
Comes bubbling up, the weeds among.
Fling broad the sail, dip deep the oar;
To sea! to sea! the calm is o'er.

To sea! to sea! our white winged bark
Shall billowing cleave its watery way,
And with its shadow, fleet and dark,
Break the caved Tritons' azure day,
Like mountain eagle soaring light
O'er antelopes on Alpine height.
The anchor heaves! the ship swings free!
Our sails swell full! To sea! to sea!

T his poem, *Sea Song,* by Thomas Lovell Beddoes, captures different moods of the sea. What gives the sea such power? What gives it the force to shape shorelines, alter climates, and enhance or harm the lives within its reaches? The answer is simple—the energy of motion.

If you stood blindfolded on a beach, what voices of the sea could you hear? What clues would reveal the strength and restlessness of the water before you? The dictionary defines *motion* as an act, process, or instance of changing place. It is movement in some form. But what causes motion? There must be some energy involved.

What moves energy through water? What grinds a cliff into fine sand? What brings delight to swimmers on a sunny day and terror in a storm?

What turns a rock into an island? What erases the sandcastles so lovingly built on shore? How does a message in a bottle travel a thousand miles? The answers to all of these questions lie in the energy produced by the motion of the oceans.

The beach is crowded on a hot summer day, so you decide to head for a quieter cove. As you cross the rocky point, something catches your eye. It is glistening among the seaweed and rocks. You inch toward it gingerly, trying not to cut your feet on the barnacles, and discover a concave plastic disk the size of a pizza plate. It looks like a bright yellow umbrella, with round holes and a long pink handle. What is this strange thing? You turn it over and discover a card attached to its underside. The card is sealed inside a clear, watertight cover. Maybe it's a secret message. You tear off the cover and read the card. It says you're holding a "drifter" released months before from an oceanographic ship in the Gulf Stream—hundreds of miles away from your beach. The card requests information—where, when, and how you found the drifter. Your answers will become part of a study being done by scientists from the ship.

Minds On! From the information you just read, put your imagination to work. How did that drifter travel such a great distance, and why did it take so long? How did it get from the ship to your beach? Was it floating at the surface, bumping along the seafloor, or somewhere in between? Hundreds of drifters were released at once. Why didn't they all tangle in the seaweed at your feet? Where else in the world might those other drifters be surprising beachcombers? Record answers to the above questions in your *Activity Log* on page 16. Performing the Try This Activity on this page can help you understand ocean water in motion.●

TRY THIS Activity!

Ocean Drifter

You can demonstrate and discover how objects at sea can move great distances.

What You Need
square shallow pan, water, cork, straw, *Activity Log* page 17

Fill a square, shallow pan with water. Float a cork in the corner away from you. See if you can bring the cork to you by blowing through a straw. Where will you direct the "wind?" What caused the cork to move? How did you get the cork to come to you? Record all your observations in your *Activity Log*.

What makes water move from one place to another? Even though it often appears that water in lakes and oceans is still and not moving, there are currents of water flowing in both.

In this lesson you'll study a variety of ocean water movements, including surface currents like the Gulf Stream, deep-water currents, waves, and tides. You can begin studying ocean currents by performing the next Explore Activity.

Activity!

What Causes Deep Ocean Currents?

You can develop a model to help explain what causes deep ocean currents.

What You Need

plastic shoe box
tap water
3 L hot tap water
small plastic bag
twist tie
food coloring
dropper
rock
ice cube
Activity Log **pages 18–19**

What To Do

1 Using your previous knowledge of air currents, in your *Activity Log* write a hypothesis that explains what you think causes ocean currents.

2 Fill the plastic box 3/4 full of tap water. Place it on the table.

3 Place the rock in the plastic bag. Fill the bag 1/2 full of hot water. Tie the bag closed.

4 Place the bag of hot water in one corner on the bottom of the plastic box.

5 Float the ice cube in the opposite corner from the bag.

6 Use the dropper to add 4 drops of food coloring to the water next to the ice cube.

7 Observe the food coloring carefully for several minutes.

8 In your *Activity Log,* make a drawing of what you observed.

What Happened?

1. Describe what you observed by answering the following questions—Where did the water sink? In what direction did the current flow along the bottom? Where did the water rise?
2. Now make another hypothesis as to what happened. How does this hypothesis compare to the one you made before you began the activity?

What Now?

1. How might you reverse the deep-water current?
2. Compare your model to Earth's oceans. Where are the oceans cold? Where are they the warmest?
3. In what direction do you think deep ocean currents move in the Northern Hemisphere? In the Southern Hemisphere? Why?
4. Record the answers to all questions in your *Activity Log*.

EXPLORE

What Powers Ocean Currents?

*I*n the Explore Activity just completed, you created a convection current. **Convection currents** are currents driven by density differences. These types of currents may occur in air or water. You noticed in the activity that the water sank at the end where you placed the ice cube, and rose where you placed the bag of hot water. Have you ever made pudding or boiled water on the stove? As water is heated from below, the water closest to the heat source warms first. As in the activity, warm water is less dense than cold water. Cooler water toward the top sinks because of its greater density and the pull of gravity. It flows under the warm water rising from the bottom.

In cartoons you often see people sending and receiving messages in bottles floating from place to place on the ocean surface. You may have observed a stick or another object floating in the ocean or a lake. The object appears to have two motions. It bobs up and down as the waves pass by, and it moves slowly and steadily in one direction. What causes these two types of motions?

What is an ocean current? An **ocean current** is a sustained movement of ocean water.

Ocean currents move horizontally across the body of water, moving water from one location to another.

A horizontal current moves across the surface. A current travels through an ocean like a river, changing the location of water caught up in its flow. Ocean waves have a vertical motion. They pass through water, making it bob up and down as energy is transmitted. But once the wave has passed, the water remains in its original location. Think of the way you move in an inner tube when a wave passes by. You bob up and down, but stay in place. If you were caught up in a current, you and your inner tube would be swept downstream.

Some currents flow along the surface of oceans, much like a stream or river flows on land. Other currents flow at great depths near

the ocean floor. There are other currents that flow between the surface and the bottom.

Most major ocean currents are powered by the wind and are called wind-driven currents. The wind blows across the surface of the ocean and pushes on the water. This friction between the wind and water sets the water in motion. **Fetch** is the distance of open water over which wind blows. The stronger the wind and the greater the fetch, the greater the resulting friction is that sets waves and currents in motion.

Winds generally affect only the upper 100 to 200 meters (330 to 660 feet) of seawater. The flow of the wind-driven currents, however, can reach down to depths of 1,000 meters (3,300 feet) or more. You may have observed this with a fish tank. When you move your hand around the surface water, the particles in the sand at the bottom of the tank rise up and move about like puppets on strings in response to the motion of your hands.

Wind-driven currents move in enormous circular patterns called gyres. These gyres don't follow the direction of the wind exactly because of Earth's rotation. In the Northern Hemisphere, Earth's rotation causes currents to bear off to the right

of the wind. Below the equator, in the Southern Hemisphere, the currents turn slightly to the left of the wind. This effect of Earth's rotation on the flow of currents is called the **Coriolis** (kōr′ ē ō′ ləs) **effect.**

Earth's general wind circulation produces the major currents of the world, such as the Gulf Stream, the Kuroshio, the California Current, the Peru Current, and the West Wind Drift. The West Wind Drift is the strongest current in the ocean. It's also the only one that circles Earth (see page 55).

From satellites transmitting temperature-sensitive photographs of the world's oceans, these great currents appear as twisting paths of bright colors within the surrounding water. Sometimes these swirls of water will break off from the main flow of the current and form a whirlpool curling in the opposite direction from its parent stream. In satellite photos, these individual whirls of water show up as dots of color, like freckles on the ocean.

Satellite maps of ocean currents help scientists understand the oceans' role in the global environmental picture.

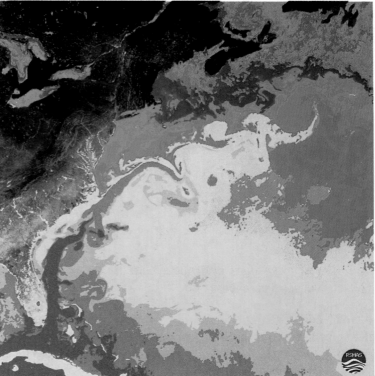

Wind produces the roughly circular currents of water across the surface of the globe and also affects the movement of water below the surface. This happens through a phenomenon called upwelling. **Upwelling** is the rising up of colder, deeper waters to replace the water blown away. Upwelling occurs when winds cause surface waters near a coast to move offshore. The upwelling of deeper waters brings nutrients to tiny plants along the coast. Fish and other marine animals flourish in these areas because of the abundance of food. In fact, half the world's fish catch comes from areas where upwelling occurs regularly. The coasts of Peru and northwestern Africa are two of the richest upwelling areas in the world. **Downwelling** is the sinking of surface waters near a coast. Regions of downwelling lack nutrients and support little marine life.

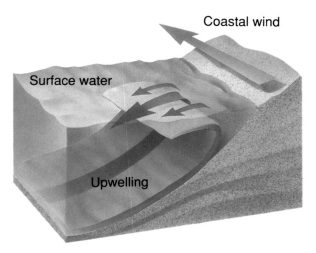

Upwelling brings deeper, colder water to the surface.

Just as you saw in the Explore Activity on pages 50–51, currents are also affected by properties in ocean water itself. Deep-water currents are caused by differences in water density. Cold ocean water with a high salinity is very dense. Warm ocean water diluted by tropical rainfall is lower in density. What effect does density have on ocean currents? Completing the next Try This Activity should help you answer this question.

TRY THIS

Activity!

Ocean Current

You can make a model of an ocean current produced by density differences.

What You Need

clear plastic pail, food coloring, sheet of plastic wrap, drinking glass, pencil, rubber band, warm and cold water, *Activity Log* **page 20**

Fill the plastic bucket 2/3 full of cold water. Fill the drinking glass full of warm water. Add food coloring to the warm water. Using a rubber band, securely fasten a sheet of plastic wrap over the top of the glass. Gently set the glass of warm water upright on the bottom of the bucket, underwater. Use your pencil to poke a small hole in the plastic wrap "lid" of the glass. Observe carefully. Make a three-step diagram in your *Activity Log* showing everything you did as well as what happened. Explain what caused the changes you observed.

Temperature and salinity are driving forces of ocean currents. Thermohaline (thûr mō hā′ lēn) circulation is the name for currents occurring when colder, saltier water sinks and pushes water ahead of it that is warmer and less dense. This is a type of deep-water circulation. Thermohaline circulation produces great vertical currents that flow from the surface to the ocean floor and back.

These currents begin in the polar regions, move along the seafloor, and then rise back to the surface. In the polar regions, the surface water becomes colder and saltier. As the ocean water freezes, salt is pushed out of the freezing water and into the surrounding water. Being colder and saltier makes the polar water more dense, so it sinks toward the ocean bottom. Once on the bottom, this water creeps slowly toward the equator. The warmer surface waters near the equator are moved away by wind and currents. The cooler water pushes up from below, replacing it.

The Gulf Stream carries warm water from the Caribbean Sea northward along the eastern coast of the United States. Other surface currents flow toward the equator carrying cooler water.

Look at the world map of ocean currents on this page. The relative temperatures of the water in these currents are indicated. Note the major currents and their relative temperatures. What general statements can you make about the relative temperatures of currents flowing along the eastern coastlines of southern Africa? What do you notice about the currents flowing along the western coastlines of the continents? Look carefully at the currents in the Northern Hemisphere. Study the patterns in the Southern Hemisphere. How are these patterns different?

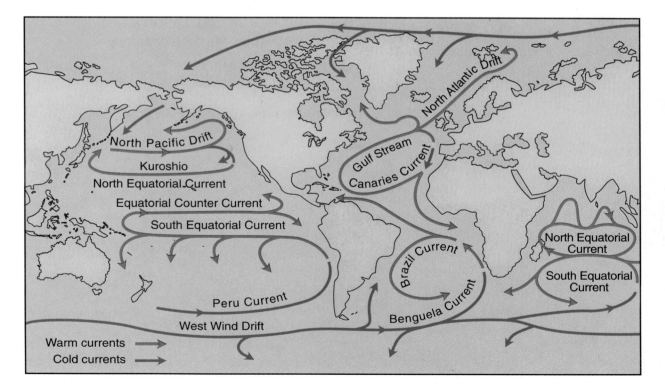

World current patterns differ from Northern to Southern Hemispheres.

Ocean Waves

The ocean is in constant motion produced by the interaction of wind, waves, tides, and currents. Waves are energy carriers. Think of the surfers riding the crests of breaking waves. Think of the thumping crash of waves breaking on a beach. During storms the waves are larger and carry even more energy.

Wind causes most of these waves. You know that you can make ripples in a pan of water by blowing on the surface. Winds blow on the ocean's surface with more force and over a longer period of time. The longer and harder the winds blow, the bigger the waves become. The waves continue for hundreds of kilometers and even continue after the wind has stopped. Look at the diagram showing the parts of a typical ocean wave. Remember that as waves move they transfer energy, but not matter.

Ocean waves slow down as they move from deep water into shallow water. As they slow down, the crests, the highest parts of a wave, get closer together. This causes the crests to become steeper until they fall over. We say the wave "breaks" near the shore. This is called **surf.** The area where the wave breaks is called the surf zone. The energy of breaking waves interacts with beach and shoreline materials. Slow, steady wave action along a beach transports sand and shell bits onto the beach where they are deposited. Large, high-energy waves pick up and carry beach material away, leaving eroded and rocky beaches. Severe storm waves have enough force to move large rocks, undercut cliff areas, and destroy homes.

Many waves generally approach the beach at an angle. The waves run diagonally up onto the beach, and then the water flows straight back. This repeated interaction between the shoreline and the breakers—the surf— moves sand down the beach in the same direction. The action of water waves can change a shoreline. They can break up exposed rock and form beaches.

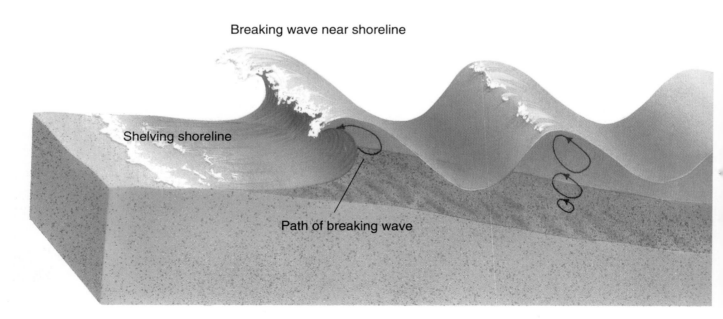

Breaking wave near shoreline

Shelving shoreline

Path of breaking wave

Water waves transfer energy, but not matter, as they move from deeper to shallow water.

Some water waves strike the beach at an angle.

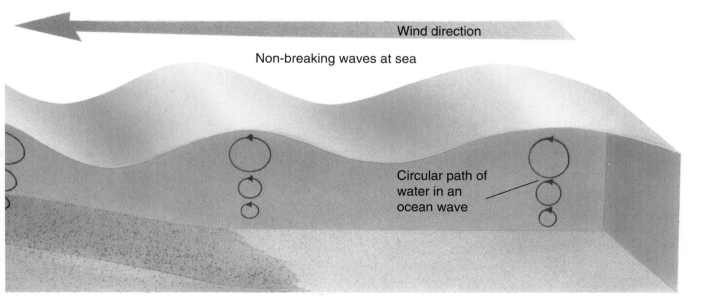

Wind direction

Non-breaking waves at sea

Circular path of water in an ocean wave

Sudden undersea movements like earthquakes or volcanic eruptions can produce a very long wave called a **tsunami** (tsü nä′ mē), or a seismic sea wave. A tsunami results from very rapid raising or lowering of an area of ocean bottom. Water rushing in or out of this area sets off the wave. A tsunami also can be produced by underwater landslides. Huge deposits of soft mud and sediment cover the steep slopes of the continental shelf. If millions of tons of sediment slip down suddenly, it gives the water a tremendous push.

Tsunamis have extremely long wavelengths, as much as 240 kilometers (150 miles) long, and they move with high speeds. In the deep waters of the Pacific, a tsunami may travel nearly 960 kilometers (600 miles) an hour! When traveling, a tsunami is hard to see, but as it comes close to shore its speed slows down and its height builds. The tsunami may suddenly rise into a wave 3 to 30 meters (10 to 100 feet) high. These large waves can be devastating to coastal regions and communities. Tsunami warning networks are operated for people living along the coastline of the Pacific Ocean. When a warning is sounded, people are alerted of potential danger and can move to higher ground.

How can you tell if a tsunami is approaching? If you're standing on the beach, with waves moving in and out regularly, things are normal. If the water suddenly pulls back a great distance like a gigantic low tide, causing fish and boats to be stranded on the beach, watch out! This retreat of water is really the trough, the lowest part, of a tsunami wave that may be only ten minutes away from hitting shore.

Tides

The rise and fall of ocean levels is called a **tide.** Tides are caused by the pull of gravity between Earth and the moon. This mutual gravitational pull causes ocean water to bulge outward on the side of Earth facing the moon. On the opposite side, Earth itself is being pulled toward the moon, causing water levels on that side to "rise." At the same time, Earth itself is being pulled away slightly from the water above it on the opposite side of Earth from the moon. Therefore, two bulges form in the oceans, one facing the moon and one on the side of Earth opposite the moon. A certain place on Earth moves through these bulges as Earth rotates. This causes the water level to rise at this place. This is called **high tide.** As the place moves out of the bulge, the water level goes down. This is called **low tide.** The tidal bulge is like the crest of a very large wave that would seem to travel around the world as Earth rotates.

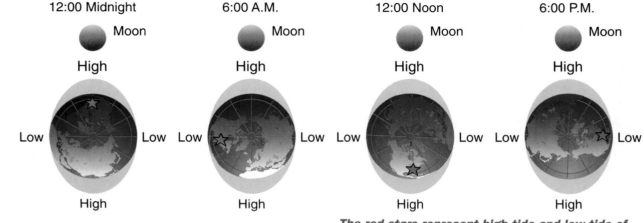

| 12:00 Midnight | 6:00 A.M. | 12:00 Noon | 6:00 P.M. |

The red stars represent high tide and low tide of the Atlantic Ocean near New York City at 12:00 midnight, 6:00 A.M., 12:00 noon, and 6:00 P.M.

A tsunami can rise as high as 30 meters (100 feet) into the air.

Tides are also affected by the shape and size of the ocean basin. Most places on Earth have two high tides and two low tides each day. But, because of the shape of the ocean basin, some places have one high and one low tide each day. In some places, it's hard to see the difference between high and low tide. In other places, there can be a 15-meter (50 foot) difference in sea level.

The height of the tides also depends on the position of the sun, moon, and Earth. The moon is always dominant. During the full and new moon phases, the gravitational pull of the sun and moon are in the same direction. At these times high tide is very high and low tide is very low. These are called spring tides. During the first and last quarter phases, the sun and moon pull at right angles to one another. At these times there is little difference between high and low tide. These tides are called neap tides. Although the gravitational attraction between Earth and sun affects ocean tides, the sun is much farther away from Earth than the moon. As gravitational attraction becomes weaker with distance, the sun has less effect on tides than the moon.

High tides can be 15 meters (50 feet) above low-tide levels.

Low tides often occur twice during the day.

Ocean Technology and You

Oceanography is a modern science that has very old roots. People have been exploring the oceans since the earliest sea voyages. Today, only a few large, highly organized institutions conduct oceanographic research on a large scale. Many voyages consist of exploration, chemical and biological research, and weather investigations. Have you ever considered living and working on the ocean?

Language Arts Link

Living on the Ocean

Imagine you are living and working on an oceanographic ship, and your family back home wonders what life is like on an ocean ship. They want to know what you see in different parts of the world. What marks the passage of time and place as the ship moves across the liquid surface of Earth? In your *Activity Log* on page 21, write a series of postcards to your family or friends. Tell them what you are observing about life on the ocean. Focus on observations such as currents, waves, and tides.

As human populations increase, the demand for power grows every day. Dwindling fossil fuel supplies make it necessary to turn to other sources for answers to this growing need. The natural motion of the ocean is providing one solution.

Hi Mom & Dad!
Tomorrow we will explore the Marianas Trench in a submersible! Miss you all! Love, Adele

Mr. & Mrs. Steven Riddle
1835 Scienceville Circle
Portsmouth, OH
43172

Life on the ocean can be both a learning and enjoyable experience.

Tidal Power

*I*n order to generate electricity, high dams are built as barricades to flowing water. This develops a huge head of water behind the dam that, when released, drives the turbines that generate power. But there is one body of water that creates a head of its own twice a day—the sea. This natural head is formed as the tide rises and falls. By building a barrier across the mouth of a tidal basin, the ebb and flow of the tide can be harnessed and used to generate electricity.

In 1966 France opened the world's first working tidal dam, the Rance. The two most important requirements of a tidal power project are a large rise and fall of water and some way of holding the water back. The Rance River estuary on the coast of Brittany is ideal in both respects. An estuary is the mouth or lower course of a river where the current meets the sea and is affected by the tides. The range between high and low tide of the Rance is as much as 13.5 meters (14.8 yards), and the wide estuary is a perfect natural reservoir for storing seawater. The barrier across the estuary is hollow. Inside are all the machinery and workshops required to run the dam. The top of the dam is a bridge road for passing motorists. Fishing and pleasure boats can pass through by way of a lock and drawbridge.

The Rance power project was an experiment initially. It has been a success, and now tidal power plants are being built in other places around the globe. However, the amount of electricity generated is never great, and it is produced only when the tide is flowing. It cannot be adjusted to meet fluctuating demands on electricity by human populations.

Tidal plants are expensive to build. The Rance dam cost $110 million in 1966. There are also few places with estuaries large enough to store adequate water, together with a tidal range of more than 10 meters (11 yards).

As the tide rises, water flows through the open gates of the dam and into the estuary. As it flows, it drives the 24 turbines set into the dam. The estuary gradually fills up until high tide is reached. Then the water level is the same on both sides of the dam, and water is no longer flowing in either direction. With no water flowing, the turbines are still.

At the height of high tide, the gates of the dam are closed. As the tide goes out, the water level on the ocean side of the dam drops. Then water is allowed to flow through the concrete tunnels of the dam, back toward the sea in the opposite direction of its earlier movement. The turbines start turning again. They are built to generate electricity no matter which direction the water flows.

Tidal power plants are also controversial. Some people think they are the "wave" of the future in generating power. Other people feel the losses outweigh the advantages. They say tidal plants are inefficient, the cost is too high for the energy produced, and the potential is great for damaging or destroying delicate plant and animal species in the areas to be flooded. Why do you think tidal power is the "wave" of the future?

Minds On! Pretend that you are part of a debate on this topic. In your *Activity Log* on page 22 , explain your views as to why tidal power plants are good or bad, beneficial or harmful.●

Tidal power plants, are expensive to build as well as controversial.

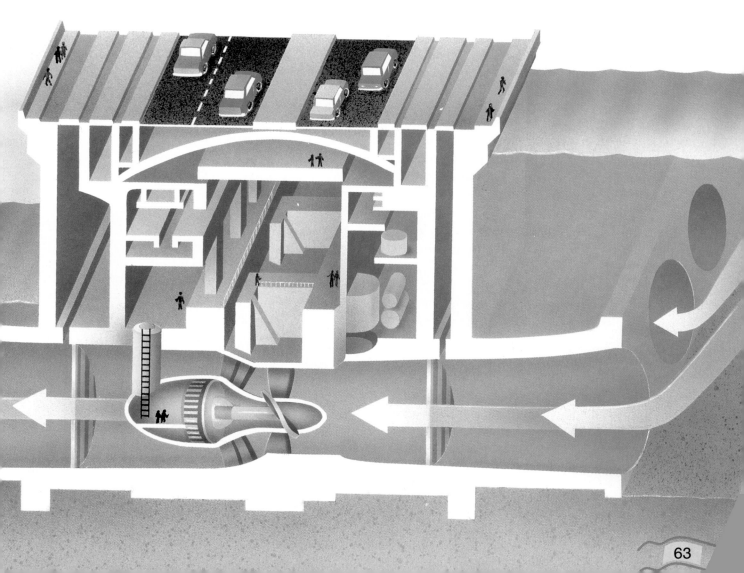

Earlier in this lesson we discussed the interaction of waves, tides, and currents within the ocean. As you read on the previous pages, tidal power has been used to generate electricity. However, the oceans affect us in other ways. Scientists are undertaking the largest research program ever begun to try to understand how the world's oceans work, and how their tiniest inhabitants regulate Earth's air and weather.

"Engines" of Weather

*O*ver the next decade, buoys and balloons will be deployed by a group of international scientists. These will study tropical oceans as "engines" of weather. Remote sensing devices and chemical tracers will be released to track ocean currents at the surface, and at depths several miles down, to better understand how energy is transferred throughout Earth's oceans. Undersea volcanoes and deep-sea vents will be probed and studied to see their effect on the ocean. One of the most difficult aspects of this study will be charting the complete cycle of nutrients, such as nitrogen, phosphorus, and carbon, through the sea.

Researchers predict that minute changes in the biological productivity of marine plants can have a large impact on climate. These tiny ocean plants are responsible for much of the oxygen we breathe. They're critical players in the world's climate puzzle. If the environment changes dramatically, these plants may respond either with a tremendous growth spurt or a massive dieback. The National Aeronautics and Space Administration (NASA) is beginning to use satellites to study plankton growth in the oceans. These satellites can

observe the colors in the sea, detecting chlorophyll and productivity in the oceans. This information will enable scientists to better understand this very important piece of the global environmental picture.

For the first time, the oceans will be approached as a single, giant integrated global circulatory system, capable of distributing life-giving heat and nutrients around the planet. As one scientist said, "Now we can begin to talk about the whole puzzle."

Literature 🐸 Link

The Voyage of the Frog

*A*fter reading the book *The Voyage of the Frog* by Gary Paulsen, pretend that you are David and you are sailing alone across the Pacific. To record your experiences, you decide to keep a diary. Write five entries in your diary describing your many experiences while aboard the *Frog*. In your final entry, include any important concepts you've learned in this lesson as a part of your experiences. Bind your entries together and design a cover for your diary.

Sum It Up

In this lesson you have studied motions within the ocean system. This constant movement is due to the ceaseless interaction of waves, currents, and tides that keep ocean water in constant motion. These interactions within the ocean system help transfer energy, maintain a somewhat uniform salinity, and bring deposited nutrients back to the surface and into the ocean ecosystem. You modeled currents, studied the natural causes of waves and tides, and learned about the effects of water motion on life in the sea and the shapes of shorelines. New technologies are constantly being developed to monitor and harness the energy and the productivity of the oceans so vital to Earth.

Using Vocabulary

convection currents
Coriolis effect
downwelling
fetch
high tide
low tide
ocean current
surf
tide
tsunami
upwelling

Create a crossword puzzle using the vocabulary words from this lesson. Try using the definition of the words in a creative way.

Critical Thinking

1. What physical property of ocean water is primarily responsible for producing deep ocean currents?

2. Explain the cause of surface currents in the ocean such as the Gulf Stream.

3. How does the Gulf Stream affect the climate of areas in the North Atlantic such as Ireland and England?

4. Suppose the pull of gravity between Earth and the moon were to increase. How would that affect Earth's ocean tides?

5. How has the rising sea level around the world affected beaches and shorelines?

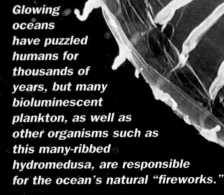

Glowing oceans have puzzled humans for thousands of years, but many bioluminescent plankton, as well as other organisms such as this many-ribbed hydromedusa, are responsible for the ocean's natural "fireworks."

Life in the Ocean

Many different kinds of plants and animals live in ocean systems. In this lesson you will learn more about their role, where they live, what they eat, and how humans interact within an ocean environment.

There are places on Earth where you can take a midnight walk along a beach. The tide is out. As you walk on the wet sand, your footprints shimmer with pale green light. You stoop at the softly lapping water's edge and run your hand through the liquid. Five ribbons of sparkling light follow your fingers. A boat drifts and tugs at its mooring line. As the rope rises from the water, drops of pale fire fall into the sea. What is going on? What is causing these natural fireworks?

The creature most often responsible for this glorious display of night light is called a dinoflagellate (dī nō flaj' ə lāt). It is a microscopic organism so small that literally billions float at the edge of a single strand of beach. They range from the tropics to the polar regions, and glow when someone or something disturbs the water.

Certain types of dinoflagellates produce a red pigment. When these organisms reproduce rapidly, they create a floating mass known as a "red tide." A quart jar of "red tide" would contain between one million and 20 million tiny red organisms! Red tide can be so thick with dinoflagellates that it smothers the marine life around it. Large numbers of fish are killed because of lack of oxygen, sunlight, and food. Clam flats are closed and businesses suffer, as people along the coast wait for the red tide to end.

Dinoflagellates are just one of the countless forms of life in the sea. The oceans of the world teem with organisms, some vast in size, others only microscopic. Their lives are interconnected and their survivals are linked. However, their influence reaches well beyond the surface of the water. Without life in the sea, we could not exist. You can simulate the light produced by marine organisms by doing the next Try This Activity.

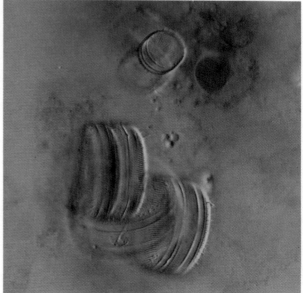

Many plankton are bioluminescent.

The interaction of many organisms exists within
this coral reef located near Pemba, Africa.

Activity!

Sea Light, Sea Bright

You can model how some sea creatures may produce light.

What You Need

empty coffee can, sheet of notebook paper, sheet of construction paper, phosphorescent paint, scissors, tape, black marker, dark room, flashlight, *Activity Log* page 23

Before you begin this activity, research and prepare a report on a marine organism that produces light. Using the empty coffee can from your teacher, trace a circle using the bottom of the can onto a piece of white notebook paper. Draw an outline of your organism within this circle with the black marker. Using the phosphorescent paint, color the parts of the organism that produce light. Cut out the circle and tape it to the inside bottom of the coffee can. Line the inside of the can with a colored piece of construction paper. Go into a dark room and shine a flashlight through the open end of the can. Observe what happens to the organism when you turn the flashlight off. How does your organism compare to the organism you researched? In your *Activity Log,* draw your organism, labeling the part responsible for producing light. Also, write a report on your organism describing other features it has that allow it to live successfully in the ocean environment.

Minds On!

Study the photograph of the coral reef carefully. Within the coral reef many different components interact with one another. Each of the living things in a coral reef requires energy. What is the primary source of energy for this system? What are some of the interactions within this system? How long might this type of environment survive? What might produce changes that could upset its balance and cause problems, or destroy it altogether? Answer all questions in your *Activity Log* on page 24.●

Earth's oceans are similar to the system existing within a coral reef or in an aquarium in your school. However, it is much more complex. Organisms within the ocean are interdependent. The next Explore Activity will give you some insight into this complex, yet exciting world of ocean life.

Sharks prey upon smaller animals in an ocean environment.

Activity!

A Web of Dependency

There are many food chains and food webs in Earth's oceans. In this activity you will construct a food chain and demonstrate how this is part of a larger food web system.

What You Need

small colored ball of yarn
food chain role cards
8 index cards
string
Activity Log **pages 25–26**

What To Do

1 From your previous knowledge about food chains, food webs, and ecosystems, make a diagram of a simple food chain in your *Activity Log*. Identify the producers and consumers in your food chain. Explain the role of each in this simple food chain system.

2 Sort the cards from your packet into a food chain. Make a diagram of the chain in your *Activity Log*.

3 Identify the producers and consumers in your food chain and discuss their roles in this system.

4 Compare your food chain with those of other groups. Discuss the interactions between members of each food chain system.

Sea lion

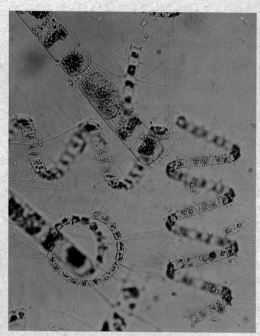

Marine phytoplankton

Krill

Killer whale

What Happened?

1. How is each food chain like a system?

2. What is the initial source of energy in each chain?

3. What is the source of organic nutrients in the ocean?

What Now?

Now, let's take a look at the relationships among the many food chains in larger food webs and ocean ecosystems. Each person in your group should pick a role card. Using the index card, write the name of the "role" you will be playing on the index card and hang it around your neck with a string. Now, with other groups in your class, form a large circle facing each other. One person from each group will have a ball of yarn of a different color. This person should throw the yarn to someone from another group that would be a part of your food chain. Follow any additional instructions given by your teacher and answer the following questions in your *Activity Log*.

1. Where does each food web begin? Explain why.

2. Which members in the ecosystem are involved in the most food webs? Explain why.

3. What happens if one member of a food web disappears?

4. Which members of the ocean food webs are competing for food?

5. At what part of a food web do you always find bacteria and nutrients? Explain why.

EXPLORE

Food Cycles in the Sea

Did you ever sing a song about an old lady who swallowed a fly? She swallowed a spider to catch the fly . . . swallowed a bird to catch the spider . . . swallowed a cat to catch the bird . . . and on and on. Pure fantasy, obviously. But there is truth behind the idea of the song. The song is about a food chain, or the path of energy flow among and between organisms. Food chains are a very real and vital part of the world's energy transfer, both on land and in the oceans.

You've probably learned about food chains and food webs that exist on land. In the Explore Activity just completed, you examined food chains and food webs (series of food chains) from the sea. The tangle of yarn tossed around the circle in your classroom clearly demonstrated how interconnected the consumption patterns are in the sea. If one link increases in number or vanishes, the entire web is affected.

Earth's oceans support life in a wide variety of ways. There are many different food chains and food webs that make up different ecosystems in a variety of ocean environments. **Ecosystems** (ek′ ō sis′ təmz) are complex systems of organisms interacting with each other and a physical and chemical environment. Each of these ecosystems is a balanced system made up of many organisms.

*The food cycle in the sea begins with plankton. **Plankton** (plangk′ tən) are tiny plantlike organisms called phytoplankton and animal-like organisms called zooplankton that float at or near the surface of the ocean.*

During photosynthesis, these phytoplankton use sunlight, carbon dioxide, water, and nutrients in the water to produce food. The zooplankton eat the phytoplankton.

These plankton in turn become food for fish and other marine animals—just like the old lady who swallowed the fly in the song.

zooplankton

When an organism dies in the sea, it begins to sink toward the ocean bottom. Before it arrives there, however, it is usually consumed by creatures dwelling at lower depths. Thus, the dead organisms are either eaten or they decay.

Live organisms give off waste products. The waste products and the remains of dead organisms are broken down by bacteria into mineral salts.

Within an ocean ecosystem, **producers** are organisms that synthesize or make food.

Producers are autotrophic (ô tə trō′ fik) organisms, usually plants or bacteria that produce food from inorganic (nonliving) substances. Plants use the sun's energy to produce food through the process of photosynthesis.

A variety of other organisms called **consumers** feed on producers.

Consumers are heterotrophic (het′ə rə trō′ fik) and are unable to make their own food to obtain energy.

Many organisms called **decomposers** break down organic tissue into vital nutrients.

Bacteria use substances such as methane gas to produce food through chemical reactions in a process called **chemosynthesis** (kē′ mō sin′ thə sis).

phytoplankton

Rising currents carry these minerals back up to the surface, where the phytoplankton use them to make food and release oxygen into the atmosphere. The food cycle is completed, ready to begin its long revolution again and again.

Life in the Sea

Environments rich in life have common requirements. In order to support life, light, dissolved oxygen, and nutrients must be available for primary producers, or plants, to carry on photosynthesis (fō' tə sin' thə sis). The products of photosynthesis are carbohydrates (food) and oxygen. These products are necessary for the survival of consumers living in the ocean environment. Primary producers thrive in shallow water or near the surface where sunlight penetrates.

Ocean water is a very stable environment since its temperature and other physical qualities vary little. Nothing similar to surface weather or climate exists below the surface. Marine plants and plantlike organisms can live only in the sunlit surface waters of the ocean, which is called the photic (light) zone. The photic zone only extends to about 100 meters (330 feet) below the surface of the water. Beyond that point, there is insufficient light to support plant life. By the time light has passed through one meter (three feet) of water, roughly half of it has been absorbed. At a depth of 100 meters (330 feet), only one percent of the surface light remains.

Some bacteria can produce organic matter from chemicals in seawater in the absence of light. These bacteria are found

Photic zone	100m
Twilight zone	1,000 m
Dark zone	6,000 m
Deepest trench	11,000 m

The amount of light at different levels of the ocean determines which organisms live there.

Large tube worms

in deep water near the ocean bottom where chemically rich hot water seeps from vents. In 1977 on a geological dive in the *Alvin*—a small, two-person submersible—scientists from the Woods Hole Oceanographic Institute made one of the most amazing discoveries of this century. Diving to the seafloor near the Galápagos (gə lä′ pə gōs′) Islands, they encountered geothermal vents that looked like chimneys spewing boiling water laden with chemicals from below the seafloor. The water was 315°C (600°F) and shot out with a force like water out of a fire hose.

The seafloor is usually a relatively barren place with little evidence of life of any kind. Around these "smokers" though, the scientists aboard *Alvin* found a teeming oasis of life—foot-long clams with blood-red bodies, ten-foot tube worms, colonies of polyps that looked like delicate dandelions, mussels, sea spiders, huge crabs, and rattail fish. The water stank like rotten eggs from the dissolved minerals spewing from the hot geysers. These unique creatures were existing through chemosynthesis, in total darkness, and miles under the surface of the sea!

Crabs

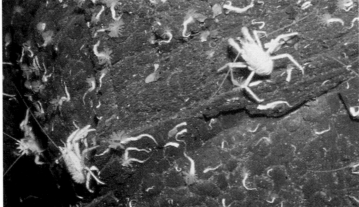

Mussels

A variety of organisms exist in the hot vents of the ocean bottom.

Scientists group types of ocean life by their marine environments. The greatest abundance of life in the ocean is found in shallow, warm waters along the continental shelf areas. Plankton drift with the ocean currents. They have very little ability to move through the water on their own. Many plankton are too small to be seen with the unaided eye. Diatoms are a common form of protistal single-celled organisms. Diatoms use sunlight to make their own food. Thus, they live in the shallow waters of the continental shelf or near the surface in deeper water. Diatoms and other protists are the most abundant form of ocean life.

Animal-like plankton feed on diatoms and other plantlike plankton. Animal-like plankton are found at all depths in the ocean. Some float freely all through their lives. Others spend only the early part of their life as zooplankton. As adults some zooplankton become strong swimmers and join the nekton grouping. The **nekton** are fish and other animals that have the ability to swim freely without the help of currents.

Larger organisms such as fish, sea turtles, dolphins, and whales swim and float near the surface. Some fish, like anchovies and herring, are herbivores and eat only plants. Others, like mackerel, tuna, and sea bass, are carnivores and eat smaller fish. Sea turtles and sea cows are herbivores and graze on plants. Still others settle to the seafloor or attach themselves to it and become part of the benthos group.

Benthos are plants and animals that live on the ocean bottom. Some, such as barnacles and oysters, attach themselves to the ocean bottom. They stay in one place throughout their lives. Some benthic organisms obtain food by filtering it from seawater or by catching nearby animals. Other shelled animals, like clams, burrow into the mud and sand on the ocean bottom, where they feed on organic nutrients in the water and mud.

Benthic plants are found on the bottom in water up to 30 meters (99 feet) in depth. Very few plants can live in deep water because of the lack of sunlight. Corals are small benthic animals that live in colonies. Corals take calcium from ocean water to build their skeletons. These calcium-rich skeletons join together in a rocklike mass called a coral reef. Coral reefs form in warm, shallow waters. The environment around coral reefs supports rich varieties of ocean life.

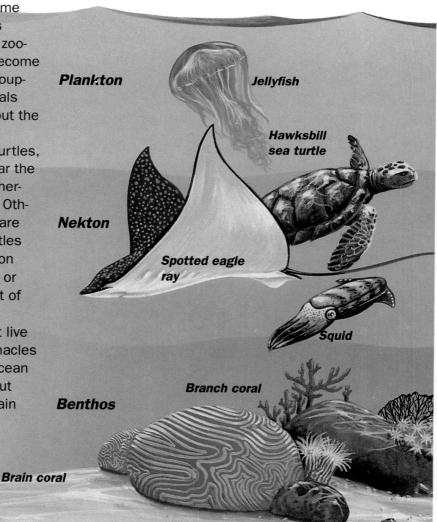

There is a diversity of life in the ocean.

Fish are the most important animals of the nekton. There are about 13,300 kinds of fish in the ocean, differing greatly in size and shape. The smallest fish, the pygmy goby, grows less than 13 millimeters (1/2 inch) in length. The largest fish, the whale shark, measures up to 18 meters (60 feet) in length. Some fish, such as mackerel and tuna, have streamlined bodies that enable them to move rapidly through the water in search of food. Other fish, like cod and flounder, have burrowing whiskers and flat bodies designed to help them feed on the seafloor.

The deep-living angler fish has light-producing organs that help it attract prey.

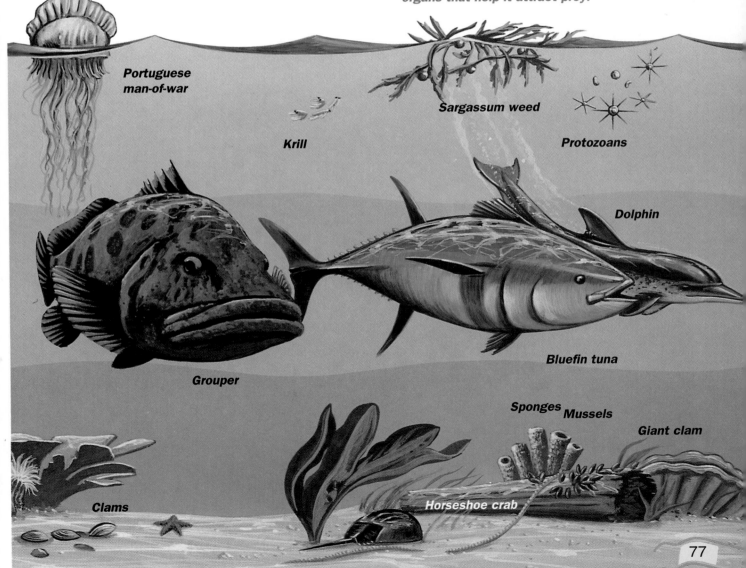

Portuguese man-of-war

Krill

Sargassum weed

Protozoans

Dolphin

Bluefin tuna

Grouper

Sponges Mussels

Giant clam

Clams

Horseshoe crab

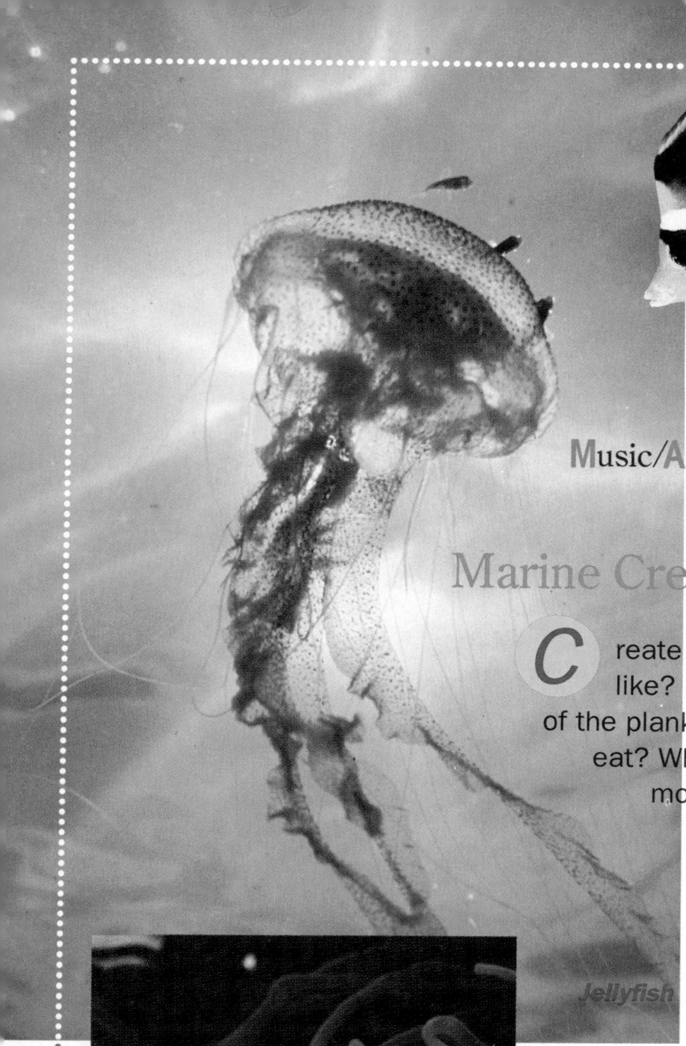

Music/Art Link

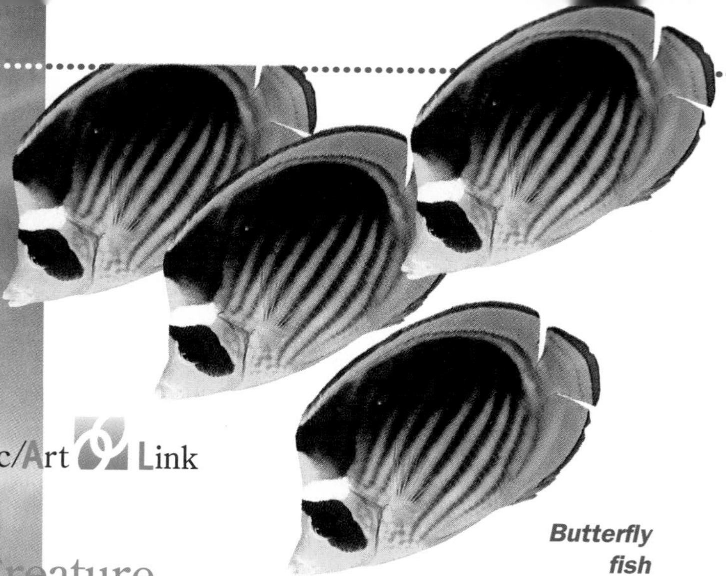

Marine Creature

Create your own marine creature. What does it look like? Is it a surface- or deep-water dweller? Is it part of the plankton, the nekton, or the benthos? What does it eat? What eats it? How does it protect itself? If it moves, what is its means of locomotion? Think about the answers to these questions before you begin, then draw your creature in your **Activity Log** on page 27. Share your drawing with other students in your class. Ask questions to see how well your classmates know the life cycles of their own creations.

Butterfly fish

Jellyfish

Clownfish in sea anemone

Tang

Marble sea star

Scientists have evidence to indicate that life on Earth began in the oceans. One of the early ocean dwellers was the bottom dweller called the trilobite (trī′ lə bīt′). Fossil evidence indicates that trilobites were abundant from about 500 to 600 million years ago. The earliest armor-plated fishes, like the one pictured on this page, appear in the fossil record during the Ordovician (ôr′də vish′ən) Period between 450 and 500 million years ago. Throughout the next 100 million years, these armor plates became thin, light-weight scales. Life is still slowly changing in modern oceans. Many organisms that existed in the past have decreased in number or become extinct. Yet, new discoveries of ancient ocean dwellers sometimes happen.

*Armor-plated fish, such as this **Dunkleosteus**, were common 450 million years ago.*

Social Studies Link

Coelacanth Discovery

The sea can yield surprises any time nets are lowered into the water. In 1938 a great event in the history of zoology occurred. A fisher off the east coast of southern Africa caught a type of fish he had never seen before. When a famous ichthyologist (ik′ thē ol′ə jist), or fish expert, saw it, he recognized it as a coelacanth (sē′ lə kanth′), a very ancient class of fish that supposedly disappeared from Earth 70 million years before! These fish were distinguished by lobed fins, forerunners of the limbs of higher animals. Zoologists from all over the world flocked to the waters there, hoping to catch another one of these incredible "extinct" fish. Fourteen years would pass, however, before another was found.

Since then, a number of coelacanths have been caught off the coast of Madagascar (mad′ə gas′kər). They are large blue fish, about 120 to 150 centimeters (4 to 5 feet) long. They can weigh as much as 80 kilograms (180 pounds). Their unusual fins are thick and scaly, unlike those of any other living fish. Bones inside the fins hinge from a single bone, like the limbs of a four-legged land animal. Their skulls are constructed like those of primitive amphibians. The fish dinners inside coelacanths' stomachs indicate that they aren't deep water swimmers. It's surprising, therefore, that these living "fossil" fish took 70 million years to appear in the net of someone who had gone fishing!

The coelacanth was thought to be extinct until 1938 when one was caught by a South African fisher.

Harnessing Ocean Ecosystems

Ocean ecosystems operate as a balancing act between life-forms and their environment. This balance can be upset by sudden changes in temperature as well as by pollution.

Sponges, algae, and other ocean creatures are yielding new substances that hold promise as medicines against cancer, parasites, and other infectious diseases like AIDS, scientists say. The search for drugs from the sea focuses on organisms that lack physical features that serve to protect most organisms from predators. These organisms don't have spines or shells, and they can't run. They appear as blobs on a reef, resembling food, yet they're not eaten. How do they manage this mysterious feat? They are protecting themselves chemically.

Marine animals hold a lot of promise as sources of new drugs. In test-tube experiments, chemists have extracted two substances from sponges that appear to be effective in combating tapeworms and other parasites that plague cattle and sheep. The chemicals also show some ability to fight viral diseases. One of them can inhibit the activity of an enzyme that causes the HIV virus, the virus that causes AIDS, to reproduce. Drugs from marine creatures are being tested now and could be on the market within the next ten years.

The oceans can be studied in many ways. All over Earth, large amounts of sewage are being poured into the ocean as well as other large bodies of water. The bacteria in the ocean is very capable of breaking down sewage and recycling it so plants and animals can use its energy source again and again. However, like anything else, the ocean has its limits. As human populations in coastal areas increase, more sewage is produced than the oceans can cope with. In some areas of the world, aquaculture engineers are trying to solve this growing problem.

Sponges, similar to this one found off Bonair Island in the Caribbean, may be a source for drugs in the future.

CAREERS

Aquaculture Engineer

How would you like to spend your day in a sewage dump? It may not sound appealing to most people, but to aquatic engineer Marlene Vector, there is nowhere more exciting to be. Marlene's goal is to find ways to transform treated sewage into sparkling clean water,

Aquatic engineers are transforming sewage into clean water through the use of aquatic lagoons.

plantlike organisms with chlorophyll—and other microorganisms that work with bacteria to break down the sewage.

Then the liquid is pumped into special tanks where artificially created marshes of plants (flowers, water hyacinths, irises, tomato plants, and eucalyptus trees) and animals (snails, striped bass, and trout) begin to eat the contaminants in the water.

The snails dine on sludge, the fish gobble up the plankton, and the plants absorb phosphorus, cadmium, and lead—all things present in the sewage broken down by the algae and bacteria. After a final cleaning in polished vats, the once-filthy liquid gushes out crystal clear after only five days. The success of this process is an amazing demonstration of nature's ability to restore itself without synthetic chemicals.

Using nets, Marlene gathers most of the organisms she needs in local streams. Then, she creates the marshes for the purifying tanks like a cook creating a stew. A little of this and a little of that...and wham!...a working ecosystem in a tank. It takes great skill to know what plants and animals to mix most effectively.

Powered by solar energy and photosynthesis, the plants and animals achieve through natural processes the same water purifying work of the huge chemical treatment plants, and at a fraction of the cost. Also, Marlene enjoys one unexpected benefit of this process. The trees and flowers that grow and flourish in the tanks can be sold to help keep the research going. But the most satisfying reward is knowing that those busy tanks of plants and animals contain one possible key to cleansing and preserving our polluted planet Earth.

brimming with healthy plants and animals. Alongside a busy sewage treatment plant surrounded by sludge lagoons, Marlene and her co-workers have built a greenhouse filled with transparent fiberglass holding tanks.

Marlene hopes to show that sewage can be treated more effectively and at lower cost by harnessing the power of normal processes found in nature, like photosynthesis. Marlene calls this process solar aquatic water purification. Raw sewage is pumped into rows of tanks containing dozens of different species of algae—tiny green, brown, or red aquatic

Diatoms: Energy Producers

What do you think is the busiest energy producer in the ocean? If you were to look at an ocean, you wouldn't see this tiny organism, but it would be all around you.

Diatoms, tiny one-celled golden algae, are found in the ocean and some fresh waters. There are hundreds of thousands of diatoms in a bucket of ocean water. Each cell is covered with a hard, glittering shell made of silica. Diatoms are the most important producers in the ocean. Tossed and churned by the constant movement of ocean currents, diatoms are kept exposed to sunlight. They use the solar energy to produce large amounts of oxygen and food for other sea life. A large humpback whale may feed on several billion diatoms every few hours!

When diatoms die, their tiny silica shells drop to the ocean floor in layers called ooze. Millions of years of buildup of these layers have made the oceans a good source for silica. Some of these layers are also found on land where the oceans once flowed. The largest deposit is in California, where layers are 420 meters (1,386 feet) thick. There, the deposits are mined for diatomite.

Diatomite is ground into powder and used to polish and clean metals. Diatomite can be used to make dynamite. It also can be used to filter liquids. The fluids are filtered through diatomite to remove dirt. Raw sugar is filtered through diatomite in the process of making table sugar. Diatomite is also used to filter fruit juices, liquid soap, and vegetable oils.

Diatoms have many important uses. Both the living organisms and their shells are used by other marine organisms.

The shells of diatoms consist of two parts that fit one inside the other.

Sum It Up

In this lesson you learned that the oceans teem with interdependent forms of life, incredibly different from one another, yet permanently connected through the food webs of the sea. You studied plankton, nekton, and benthos and how each of these organisms interact with each other in varied ecosystems of the sea. Origins of food from the sea were investigated in this lesson, and the potential of using marine organisms in tackling the problem of pollution on Earth was examined. The sea belongs to each of us. Are you willing to do your part and encourage others to do their part in preserving its resources?

Using Vocabulary

autotrophic
benthos
chemosynthesis
consumers
decomposers
ecosystems
heterotrophic
nekton
plankton
producers

Using the vocabulary words from this lesson, construct a simple crossword puzzle. Write your own definitions for the words as the "clues." Trade puzzles with your classmates to test your understanding of these words.

Critical Thinking

1. Diagram and label an ocean life food chain. Identify the producer, consumer, and decomposer.
2. Construct a chart showing common members of the ocean life groups plankton, nekton, and benthos.
3. Describe the role of decomposers in ocean food webs.
4. Why has the ocean played such an important role in the development of life on Earth?
5. What relationship exists between tiny diatoms and the large humpback whale?

Humans have always been dependent upon the oceans. Fish caught in Benoa Harbor yield a major food source for people in Bali, Indonesia.

84

Human Interaction and Dependence on Oceans

N o one person or country can claim the oceans. The oceans contain a huge variety of plant and animal life as well as many other resources. In this lesson you will be introduced to the interactions of humans and the oceans.

You have studied about oceans in this unit. You know that Earth has a limited amount of water that moves through a cycle of evaporation, condensation, and precipitation. You have also learned about properties of ocean water, that the oceans are in motion, and that they support a variety of interdependent living organisms. It is this interdependence and how humans affect oceans both positively and negatively that we will focus on in this lesson.

Oceans hold vast resources that are still being researched. As much of the world's land has already been used for agriculture and building, increasingly we will look to the oceans as a source of food to feed our people. Since more than 70 percent of Earth is water, people often seek to build on ocean shorelines with varying success. Because humans are consumers, trash and garbage is produced that needs to be disposed of in safe and sanitary ways. All of these activities may at times strain the ocean environment as we interact with it. It is important that we learn how to function responsibly as we interact with Earth's large water environment.

"Water, water everywhere but not a drop to drink." How often have you heard that quote? Fresh water is scarce in some parts of the world. Some desert countries are studying the possibility of towing icebergs to their shores as a source of fresh water. The oceans appear to have plenty of water, but none of it is suitable for human consumption. Scientists are developing increasingly effective technology to obtain fresh water from salt water. So far, however, it's still very expensive to extract large quantities of fresh water from ocean water. You will be able to try your hand at one method of freshwater extraction in the next Explore Activity.

Activity!

Fresh Water From Salt Water?

You will build a model of a solar still to convert salt water to fresh water.

What You Need

large plastic shoe box
salt water
plastic cup with lid
clear plastic wrap
marble
hand lens
straws
Activity Log **pages 28–29**

What To Do

1 Using the materials supplied by your teacher, set up a solar still to convert salt water to fresh water.

2 Keep the following factors in mind as you set up and observe your model.

a. Concentrate on your hypothesis. Think of ways you can obtain fresh water from salt water.

b. Set up your experiment to use the available materials to design a solar still that can convert salt water to fresh water.

c. Make sure that all factors in your experiment remain the same each day as you observe what happens (you begin with the same amount of water, light source is the same, and so forth).

3 Observe your solar still each hour during the day. Continue another day if needed.

4 Record all observations in your *Activity Log.*

What Happened?

1. Describe what happened inside your solar still.
2. Describe the taste of the salt water and the water you collected.
3. Follow a drop of salt water while it changes from salt water to fresh water, and explain what happens to it each step of the way.
4. How much fresh water did you obtain? How long did it take?
5. Is this enough fresh drinking water for one person for one day?

What Now?

1. How could you get enough fresh water for a one-day supply?
2. Suppose you needed to get enough fresh water for a city. What problems would you face?
3. How could it be possible to use a similar device to obtain drinking water from desert sands when survival is at stake?

EXPLORE

Ocean Resources

In the Explore Activity you did, you made fresh water from salt water. In the past, salt has been exchanged as money, tossed over shoulders for good luck, and smuggled by thieves. Salt was once considered rare and precious. With populations increasing around the globe, fresh water is becoming a priceless commodity.

Certainly one of the most valuable resources for life on planet Earth is fresh water. Some areas of the world appear to have abundant supplies of fresh water. Other areas have little or no source of fresh water. People in dry regions may become more dependent upon desalination (dē sal'ə nā' shən) of ocean water. **Desalination** is the removal of salts and other dissolved solids from ocean water. Desalination is most often accomplished by evaporation. In this process ocean water is heated until the water evaporates, leaving the salts behind. The water vapor is then cooled and condensed to a liquid.

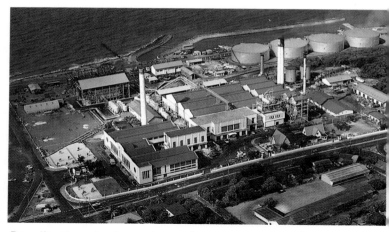

Desalination plants are becoming commonplace in many areas as the world's demand for fresh water increases.

Desalination technology is improving rapidly, but the cost of building new plants and providing the energy to power them is expensive. At this time production of desalinated water costs about twice as much as it does to get fresh water taken from other sources. Another problem with desalination is that the plants must be close to a source of ocean water. It would be far too expensive to truck seawater to inland plants.

Fresh water also can be obtained from frozen ocean water. When ocean water freezes, much of its salt content is removed. Only about one-third of

Shrimp being unloaded at the cannery dock in Homer, Alaska

Inexpensive desalination of ocean water could transform Africa's Namib desert.

the salts are taken up in the ice. The rest remain behind in the unfrozen water. Salt can then be separated from the ice by heating and condensing, leaving fresh water.

Valuable minerals are dissolved in seawater. Therefore, the by-products in the desalination process are of great value. To get large quantities of salts and minerals, ocean water is placed in large ponds on land. The water evaporates, leaving salts and minerals behind. The minerals are then collected and converted to useful products. Table salt is the most abundant mineral harvested from evaporation ponds. Ocean water salts also contain magnesium, sulfur, potassium, and bromine.

Some minerals are found on the ocean floor in ball-like lumps or nodules. Manganese, cobalt, and nickel are valuable metals found in nodules. The nodules can be collected directly from the ocean floor. Manganese is an important metal. It's used in the steel industry. Manganese removes impurities from steel to make a clean metal. It's also used in some paints, dyes, and fertilizers.

A tub of oysters freshly collected from the ocean in Bellingham, Washington

Oil and natural gas form in deposits buried on continental shelf areas. Oil drilling and production platforms are located in shelf waters off the coasts of Texas, Louisiana, California, and the northern slope of Alaska. Wells are drilled from these platforms into the oil- and gas-bearing rocks. The oil and gas are brought to shore by ships and pipelines.

People all over the world rely heavily on seafood such as fish, crabs, shrimp, and oysters. In some cases, as people become more dependent on fish for food, more fish are being taken than can be replaced by natural reproduction. Overfishing in an area, for even one year, means a shortage of fish for years to come.

Oceans provide a wide variety of foods for humans. People eat plants such as seaweed. Chemicals also are taken from seaweed and used to make foods such as ice cream and salad dressing. Kelp is harvested for food, iodine, and potassium.

An oil-drilling platform on the North Sea

There are more than five billion people on Earth today. Food resources for an ever-increasing population are a concern to sociologists and economists across the world. Our land resources have been pushed to the limit. The ocean is already a vast resource of food for many, but new sources of food from the ocean are being considered.

Imagine walking under a softly swaying forest canopy. Sunlight filters down from above, giving a golden radiance to the whole scene. Is that a rain shower sweeping in? No. It's a school of fish! You're underwater in a forest of giant Pacific kelp, the largest seaweed in the world. Seals speed by like torpedoes. A fishing pelican plunges from the air, leaving a cascade of silvery bubbles. This strange, breathtakingly beautiful world may be the restaurant of the future for people as well as marine life. Giant kelp grows in marine forests along the Pacific coast of Canada, the United States, and Mexico's Baja California. Weighing up to 135 kilograms (300 pounds) and reaching heights over 30 meters (100 feet), giant kelp can streak toward the surface at the rate of 61 centimeters (2 feet) a day! Its 15- to 18-meter (50- to 60-foot) vines move in unison with passing currents. No other marine plant grows so rapidly or restores itself so quickly.

Little, golf ball-sized bulbs of air buoy up the blades of these massive plants so they can capture the energy of the sunlight filtering through the water. Rootlike "holdfasts" keep the kelp anchored to the seabed. A single plant can be a city within itself, supporting more than a half million small marine animals of 750 different species.

To understand how kelp forests work, you have to take land botany and

Giant Pacific kelp

turn it upside down. The fronds of the kelp extract energy from the sun through photosynthesis. They absorb nutrients from the surrounding water instead of the seabed beneath them. These nutrients then travel down the plant to nourish new growth at its base. Blades at the base release billions of seedlike spores. Most are washed away, but some attach to the seabed, and new kelp plants start their race toward the surface.

Seaweed is already a billion-dollar business. In many parts of the world, brown kelp is harvested and processed into a gel-like substance called algin. A teaspoonful of algin can make a quart of water as thick as honey. Algin works as a chemical fastener, or colloid. It holds the moisture in packaged foods and medicines. It prevents products from separating or disintegrating. It is used in making ice cream to keep the water in the milk from turning into ice crystals when the ice cream is frozen. Algin goes into salad dressings, chocolate milk, and aspirin. It forms the transparent capsules around the powdery contents of pills. It also prevents toothpaste and makeup from running out of tubes.

Besides their industrial uses, various seaweeds are rich in carbohydrates and essential minerals and nutrients. They may have a strong, nutty flavor or a light, celery-like taste. In a world where hunger is growing steadily, seaweed will play an increasingly vital role in global diets. Asian and Polynesian cultures have recognized the benefits of seaweed as a food source for hundreds of years. The ancient Hawaiians used more than 40 species of limu (Hawaiian for seaweed) as a rich source of minerals and essential trace elements to balance their diet of fish and poi (a paste made from taro root).

Cultivation of seaweed is a major industry in Japan.

For many years Japanese coastal villagers cultivated nori, algae sold in purple-colored sheets. These pioneers of fishing first grew young plants on bamboo stakes and then shifted them to nets laid horizontally above the shallow seabed. In 1949 Kathleen Drew, an English botanist, identified the seaweed from which nori is made. Her discovery allowed the Japanese to "seed" their nets and extend production into deeper, cleaner waters. Today, nori production is the country's largest, single, inshore-marine industry, a billion-dollar-a-year business!

In 1972 an American scientist named Howard Wilcox first used sea algae to produce methane for use as a fuel. Besides seaweed as food, kelp—one form of seaweed also known as sea algae—is now being converted as a source for ocean-energy farms. *Methane* can be produced through bacterial decomposition of organic matter in oxygen-free containers. The methane can be economically converted to a high-quality fuel. About 868 square kilometers (347 square miles) of kelp farms could fill the fuel needs of the United States for one year! The idea consists of "harvesting" these fast-growing algae, and then having them digested by bacteria, which causes the emission of methane.

The future of seaweed as food, an energy source, and an industrial base is expanding. Its successful use will require a great deal of international cooperation, pollution control, and sharing of territorial waters and resources. Marine plants are collectors and concentrators of nutrients. Wild sea forests and ocean-energy farms may hold the key to a solar-based world food-and-energy production system in the future.

Using and Protecting Ocean Shorelines

*I*f you would travel along the east and west coasts of the United States, you would see many different types of coastlines. Traveling along the coast in Washington and Oregon, you would find rocky sea cliffs with a few small, scattered beachfronts tucked between the cliffs. However, if you drove along the shores of the Carolinas, Georgia, or Florida, you would see broad, flat, sandy beaches. Inland from these beaches you may see tall sand dunes that have formed from the blowing and drifting beach sand.

Beaches are deposits of loose material that run parallel to the shoreline. They extend toward the ocean to between 9 and 40 meters below the water. Waves and currents constantly erode and deposit materials and alter the shape of beaches. Shoreline alterations to accommodate houses, hotels, and condominiums can increase erosion and destruction of natural areas. People have built homes, hotels, highways, condominiums, and parks along the world's coastlines.

Land is constantly being lost to the ocean. Scientific research has revealed that 70 percent of the world's sandy beaches are slowly slipping into the sea. From East Anglia to the Mediterranean, and North Africa to California, every year vacationers are basking on smaller and smaller strips of sand, according to a global survey on beach regression by the International Geographical Union. This phenomenon is due to rising sea levels caused by climate change and human-induced damage.

People who live near the coast want to prevent it from changing. They want to be able to have harbors for their boats and a secure base for their homes and cottages. Over the years, people have tried to find ways to protect what they have built. They have constructed breakwaters, groins, seawalls, and jetties to try to prevent the natural course of change along shorelines. These have been costly and haven't always been as successful as people would have liked. Look at the photographs and diagrams to see the purpose for this construction and some of the problems they have caused.

Groins are short walls built at right angles to the shore to trap moving sand.

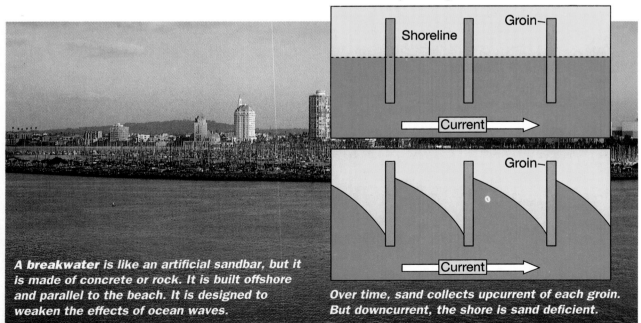

*A **breakwater** is like an artificial sandbar, but it is made of concrete or rock. It is built offshore and parallel to the beach. It is designed to weaken the effects of ocean waves.*

Over time, sand collects upcurrent of each groin. But downcurrent, the shore is sand deficient.

*Often **jetties,** barriers that are usually built in pairs, extend from the mouth of a river into the ocean. They are designed to keep drifting sand from blocking the river.*

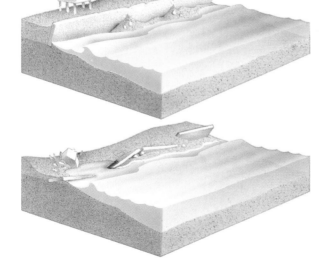

*Sometimes **seawalls,** walls built just behind the shoreline that act as artificial barriers, help keep the ocean away from the shore. Other times, artificial barriers are eroded by the natural force of ocean waves, causing shoreline property to be destroyed.*

Literature Link

Coastal Rescue:
Preserving Our Seashores

A s a part of environmental awareness week, your school is sponsoring a newspaper writing contest. After reading the book *Coastal Rescue: Preserving Our Seashores* by Christina Miller and Louise Berry, you decide to write your article on one of the following — (1) human-made problems facing our shores; (2) use of the coastline through centuries; (3) problems with making important decisions on the use and preservation of our coasts; or (4) suggestions on ways you and others in your school and community can help preserve our coastlines.

Looe Key Reef Sanctuary, Florida Keys

120-meter freighter rests on Molasses Reef after accident.

Humans are dependent upon the ocean in many ways. We have a responsibility to protect Earth's oceans and its delicate ecosystems. However, human interaction with the ocean isn't always harmful.

Human interactions can sometimes be lifesaving for complex marine ecosystems. When a 120-meter (400-foot) freighter strayed off course in 1984 near the southern tip of Florida, it crushed a huge section of an underwater coral garden called the Molasses Reef. The reef is home to countless fish, plants, and animals. The animals use the reef for survival, and in death their remains become part of the reef. The ship destroyed an area the size of a football field in this fragile, colorful realm. When the ship was towed off the reef, it caused even more damage. Concerned marine biologists decided something had to be done quickly! But they didn't know if it would be possible to bring the reef back to life.

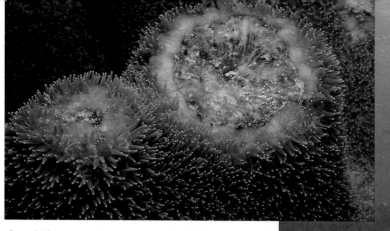

Coral tissue and algae recolonizing damaged area

A coral reef looks like a porous rock, but it is really made up of the shells and skeletons of millions of tiny animals. Inside this framework live coral polyps, each about the size of a pencil eraser. Polyps have a cup-shaped body and a mouth opening at one end of the body that is surrounded by many tentacles. As the polyps grow, they build new skeletons on top of the old, forming the reef. This formation happens over thousands of years.

Molasses Reef prior to accident

A marine biologist prepares to cement broken coral.

Ralph Lopez, a marine scientist, organized a repair team. Imagine the difficulty of working around organisms so delicate they can die from the touch of a finger! Marine biologists filmed the damaged area first. Then, using hammers and pulleys, they repositioned the giant broken coral heads—like piecing together a three-dimensional underwater living puzzle!

Using a type of glue that could work and set quickly in water, the scientists rebuilt the broken reef, piece by piece by piece. The idea behind the glue came from nature itself. Marine algae give off a substance similar to the glue used to repair the reef. It was an extremely ambitious and difficult task. However, through human effort, the coral reef is getting a second chance at life.

Human Interaction With the Ocean

During a recent storm in the Pacific Ocean, 40,000 pairs of running shoes were lost overboard from a huge cargo ship. Imagine the surprise of the fish below! As shoes began to wash up along the west coast, enterprising individuals collected them, rinsed them out, and advertised their finds—looking for people who might have found the partners to their shoes.

Not all spills are this funny, or solved with such joyful ingenuity. Far too often headlines in newspapers read: "Oil Spill Takes Big Toll on Sea Life." Oil that spills from pipelines or oil tankers first covers the surface of the water. Then it moves with the currents towards shorelines. There it coats water birds and sea creatures such as seals and otters. Surfaces of beaches and coastlines are fouled by the oil, and any that is left on the water eventually settles to the bottom. There it destroys places where sea organisms live, grow, and reproduce.

You know that oil spilled in the ocean causes much damage to the environment. It would be nice if oil spills never occurred but since they do, it is necessary to find ways to contain them or clean them up. Do the next Try This Activity to find some materials that may be useful in cleaning oil spills.

Activity!

Clean It Up!

Which materials might be the most useful in cleaning up oil spilled on water?

What You Need

5 milk cartons, plastic spoon; food coloring, water, vegetable oil, variety of materials, *Activity Log* page 30

Fill each container half full of water. Add a few drops of blue food coloring. Add a spoonful of vegetable oil to each container. Experiment with each of the materials to see which is most useful in cleaning the oil from the water. Record the results in your *Activity Log*. Which material did you find cleaned the most oil? What other materials would you like to try? Suppose you could find a way to contain the oil in a smaller area. How would that make cleanup easier?

Oil pollution presents a major problem to the fishing industry, killing thousands of fish annually.

Many oceans of the world are littered with waste.

Every year more than 14 billion pounds of trash are dumped into the oceans of the world. Over half the trash that washes up on beaches is made of plastic. Some plastics don't break down for 100 years or more! Because some plastics float, small pellets and beads of plastic are often mistaken as fish eggs or plankton by seabirds. Birds can die from eating these bits of plastic trash. The plastic rings off six-packs of canned drinks strangle seabirds and marine mammals by the thousands. In addition, some plastics contain PCBs—chemicals that cause birds to lay thin-shelled eggs that won't hatch. Sea turtles can die after eating plastic bags, mistaking them for jellyfish. The death toll on marine life from human trash is becoming worse every year.

What do you think can be done to help solve this problem?

Unsightly beach pollution

Social Studies Link

Ocean Pollution

Oceans across the world are being polluted in one way or another. Go to the library and research the oceans and seas of the world. Then choose one of the oceans that has become an area of concern because of pollution. How is this area becoming polluted? Is the pollution artificial or natural? In your report include ways pollution of this ocean is harming people, industry, and the shoreline. How is this pollution affecting the use of food and natural resources from the sea? Finally, focus on the people living in the area of this ocean. Pretend that you live in this area. List some ideas, suggestions, or ways you and others might be able to help prevent further pollution of this ocean. If you could pass a law about ocean pollution, or cleanup, what would it be? Record your observations and ideas in your **Activity Log** on page 31.

Viewing the problem of marine and environmental pollution on a global scale can be alarming. However, answers begin with small steps. Let's look at the efforts of one small group to save the salmon.

Salmon are one of the most important fish in the world for food and fishing. Most salmon live in the coastal waters of the North Pacific Ocean. Born in freshwater streams, salmon migrate into oceans for most of their lives. When the time comes for a salmon to have its own young, a salmon will return to the stream of its birth. Adult salmon swim upstream against incredible odds to accomplish this feat. They travel a long journey that takes several months.

Snohomish County, north of Seattle, has nearly 4,800 kilometers (3,000 miles) of creeks, streams, and rivers. The students of Jackson School focused their concern on Pigeon Creek, which had become very polluted. They noticed that no salmon had returned to the waters of Pigeon Creek to spawn in more than a decade. For five years the students patrolled the stream. Every day someone from the school walked its banks, looking for signs of pollution. They watched for signs of sewage runoff or litter from nearby housing developments. They appeared before a city council to argue against the construction of a sewage plant over the mouth of Pigeon Creek.

Then one day a fifth-grader on patrol discovered their long-awaited reward. A coho salmon was swimming up Pigeon Creek to spawn. Pigeon Creek is now thriving as a spawning ground for salmon returning from the Pacific Ocean. The Jackson School's Adopt-a-Creek program has become a model for other concerned community groups, schools, and neighborhood organizations across the nation.

Minds On! What environmental or water pollution problem exists in your city or town? Think of a possible solution to the problem. With several classmates, write a plan to help solve the problem. Compare your plan with that of other groups.●

People are getting the message that what they do has far-reaching effects on the rest of Earth. Humans need to be more responsible in preserving and maintaining the health and well-being of the oceans. The future of the oceans and the future of humanity are linked permanently.

Salmon swimming upstream

Sum It Up

In this lesson you examined the close interconnections between humans and the sea. You demonstrated how to obtain fresh water from seawater through a process called desalination, and examined the oceans as a potential source of food for the future. You've read about the damage of pollution and the good that can sometimes come with human intervention. Understanding the problems facing our oceans isn't enough. Protection of the oceans now will ensure their availability as a source of food for future generations. As concerned citizens of planet Earth, you can begin to undertake conservation projects to help protect our most valuable resource — the oceans — the one system that interacts with all systems for the benefit of everyone.

Using Vocabulary

beaches   **groins**
breakwater   **jetties**
desalination   **seawalls**

The title of this lesson is "Human Interaction and Dependence on the Oceans." Explain what this means using the vocabulary words of this lesson.

Critical Thinking

1. Why is making fresh water in desalination plants expensive? What are some of the by-products of desalination? Can you think of a way that both benefits could be gained from one process?

2. If you worked for a large oil company as an environmental engineer, how would you prepare for possible oil spills? Include the equipment, materials, and numbers of people you would need.

3. Suppose you lived near a pond. One day you noticed a number of dead fish floating on it. What would you do to determine the cause of the kill? List the process you would use and the steps you would take to prevent this from happening again.

4. Large oceangoing ships have problems with trash and garbage buildup while they are at sea. What systems would you propose they use to prevent dumping their waste overboard?

5. What could you and your classmates do on a small scale to help conserve Earth's water resources? Work with three others to devise a plan that you could carry out. Present it to the rest of the class. If you tried it for a month, what would you accomplish?

Unusual Ocean Experiences

*I*n this unit you have explored Earth's oceans, the chemical and physical properties of ocean water, its motion and circula– tion, the varied and dynamic seafloor features and topography. You have seen graphic illustrations of life in the ocean, balanced ecosystems, and finally the impact of human interaction and dependence on the oceans. Because of its oceans, Earth is unique among all planets in the solar system.

Although people have always been interested in the oceans, it was not until rather recently that they have been able to answer simple questions such as: How deep is the ocean? What does the ocean floor look like? How do currents affect the climate of some regions? What effect do humans have on the oceans? Natural curiosity and improved technology allow us to learn more each day about the oceans, their resources, and human impact upon this complex Earth system.

CAREERS

Whale Song Saver

*R*osa Santiago is studying the marks on a long strip of paper. Some are thick, some thin, some are long and wavering, others are short as dots. They all look like pencil smudges against the light paper. But Rosa is singing as her fingers trace the marks, changing her songs from sounds like "woo, woo, yup" to moans and chirps and grunts. Recording instruments fill the room around her. Headphones dangle around her neck. Is it a recording studio? Is Rosa learning to play a bizarre new instrument? No. Rosa is singing the song of a whale. Humpback whales swim and feed in cool waters all summer. In the win-

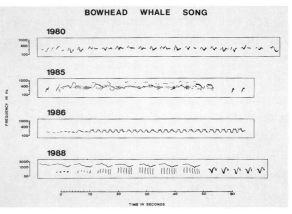

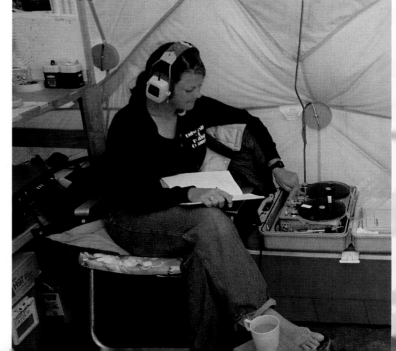

The top illustration shows spectrograms of ten consecutive songs of a bowhead. The second one shows one example of the song from four different years. Bowheads, like humpbacks, sing a different song every year.

ter, they move to warmer waters to mate and give birth—and sing!

Rosa's been studying and analyzing whale songs for years. She spends her winters on boats in the waters around Hawaii and Bermuda, listening to and recording the humpback whales' beautiful songs. By lowering hydrophones, underwater microphones, into the water, the sounds are picked up and recorded on tape.

Birds, frogs, and other animals sing, but their songs are short, with only a few simple patterns. The song of a humpback can last from five minutes to a half hour. Because the sounds have elaborate, repeated patterns, they are truly songs.

Rosa transfers the sounds recorded by the hydrophones to a machine called a spectrum analyzer. It translates the sounds into visual pictures on a screen and paper tape. The patterns change as the sound changes. They jump up if the pitch is high, and fall if the pitch is low. They become darker if the sound grows

The humpback whale is not only graceful, but also sings beautiful songs.

loud, and paler if the sound gets softer. The marks on the paper spectrogram are the "notes" of the whale's song.

Rosa studies the spectrograms carefully, looking for groups of patterns called "themes." At the beginning of winter, all humpback whales in one area sing the past winter's song. By the end of the winter, they all sing a different song, but they all sing the same new one! No other animals change their songs this way. Are the humpback whale songs territorial? Are they mating calls, or are they simply the sounds of joy? By studying the songs of these marine composers, Rosa Santiago hopes to find the answer.

Rosa Santiago enjoys her job as a whale song saver.

A Tale of Three Whales

n October 1988 a remarkable thing happened. Humans stepped into a dramatic struggle with nature—and helped the survivors. On the morning of October 7, 1988, Roy Ashmaogak (the Mayor of North Slope Borough, Alaska, and an Inuit whale hunter) left his home in the small town of Barrow. He walked in the early morning light, scouting the edge of the ice pack for bowhead whales. The weather was bitterly cold. Winter had come early, and the sea around Barrow had already frozen over. But Roy had lived in Barrow all his life, so he was accustomed to the freezing temperature and to being surrounded by ice and snow for months on end. He had hunted for seals in conditions like these many times.

As Roy tramped across the ice, something caught his eye. As he moved closer, he saw an unbelievable sight. Three California gray whales were pushing their great heads through a crack in the ice! They were frightened, bruised, and bleeding from bashing against the ice—trying to breathe. If the hole froze shut, the whales would have no air.

Roy knew at once that the whales were trapped. Ice was everywhere and was closing in fast behind the whales. Every minute lost in finding help meant more ice trapping these

A Barrow, Alaska native was the first to discover the trapped whales.

strays. He suspected that the three whales had been left behind when the rest of their herd began its long migration south from their summer feeding grounds in the Arctic Ocean to their winter feeding grounds in the warm waters of California.

Surprised by the sudden early arrival of winter, they seemed to have lost their sense of direction. Instead of heading for the open water, they entered a shallow bay where the water had quickly frozen over and formed a wall of ice at the bay's mouth. There was no way out. The whales were also growing weary from constantly swimming against the currents of water under the ice, tugging them away from the air hole. The whales were young, one two-year-old and two one-year-olds. Young whales are often sent ahead as scouts before an advancing pod.

Whales need to come up to the surface about every four minutes to breathe. Roy knew something had to be done soon to help the whales. The whales had managed to make one small breathing hole, but the ice was thick, and they were too weak to create any additional holes. Roy raced back to Barrow to look for help.

At first people listened without taking action. Some felt it would be interfering with nature to help the whales. If they were silly enough to get lost, they shouldn't be helped. But others began to feel differently. Someone commented, "It's like going out and freeing Bambi." The story of the whales hit the local newspapers and appeared on television...then spread further and further around the globe. The Inuit people of Barrow trooped onto the ice with chainsaws and pickaxes to cut more breathing holes for the whales and guide them through to open water.

Before long, people everywhere knew of the plight of the three whales. Scientists and concerned individuals flocked to Barrow to see what could be done. But was it too late? By now, the Inuit had worked for 14 days and nights to cut a line of breathing holes in the ice, leading toward the sea. But the holes kept freezing over and the whales seemed too frightened to follow the trail. To make matters worse, the youngest whale, nicknamed Bone, was ill. It was wheezing with pneumonia and trying to rest its head on the ice shelf. On Friday, October 21, it died.

Freezing temperatures made efforts to rescue the trapped whales near Barrow, Alaska a monumental task.

Many rescue attempts, such as the use of this sky-crane helicopter, failed to free the trapped whales.

The two remaining whales, nicknamed Crossbeak and Bonnet, were tiring. Something had to be done quickly if they were to escape from their ice prison. An enormous ice barge, which looked like a gigantic bulldozer, tried to smash a path through the ice, but it stuck in mud. Then a sky-crane helicopter hammered the ice with a concrete weight. It punched a line of holes from the whales to the ice wall at the mouth of the bay, but Crossbeak and Bonnet would not move. The rescuers were frantic.

Plans were drawn up to airlift the whales to safety in a huge net slung from a helicopter! This had the potential of being very dangerous for both the people and the whales. It had never been tried before and a California gray whale, although not the largest of whales, still weighs about 30,000 kilograms (66,000 pounds). Another suggestion involved the use of dynamite. But experts feared the blasts could hurt the sensitive hearing of the gray whales and other marine mammals nearby. "If we made them deaf,

we'd never get them out," one of the rescuers said.

Then, on the 20th day—Wednesday, October 26—just as everyone had almost given up hope, a Russian icebreaker sailed to the rescue. All day and all night, the huge ship charged at the ice. By the morning of the following day, part of the ice wall at the bay's mouth had been destroyed and a clear, narrow channel led from the whales to the open sea.

At first the whales hesitated. They seemed reluctant to leave the sounds of the chainsaws around them. They had come to associate that sound with air holes and breathing—their lifeline of the past weeks. Finally, they turned and headed out to sea.

"It looks good," said Roy Ashmaogak, as he stepped from a search plane the next morning. "It looks like they have moved on." The exhausted and jubilant rescuers collected their equipment and returned to their homes around the world.

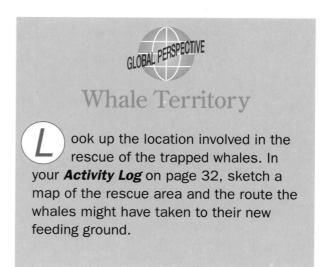

GLOBAL PERSPECTIVE

Whale Territory

L ook up the location involved in the rescue of the trapped whales. In your *Activity Log* on page 32, sketch a map of the rescue area and the route the whales might have taken to their new feeding ground.

Think about all of the interactions among the living and nonliving parts of the oceans you have studied in this unit. Many factors are at work in every segment, and a change in any one factor can have a harmful impact on some part of the environment. Keep these factors in mind when you do the Try This Activity.

TRY THIS

Activity!

Undersea Ecosystem

You will design your own undersea ecosystem.

What You Need

Activity Log page 33

Imagine having the opportunity to design your own human undersea ecosystem or habitat. Where would you place it? In what ocean would it be? At what depth is it? What is the temperature of the environment? What would be the purpose of your habitat? Would it be a community designed to ease overcrowding on the continents above or would it be a scientific research station? If your habitat has a scientific purpose, what questions or problems would the researchers aboard be investigating? How long could they remain below the ocean's surface? Would it be possible to go outside the habitat to explore nearby ocean conditions directly? Would your habitat have a globally diverse population? If so, what laws, regulations, and accommodations would you pass to ensure its safe and peaceful operation? Describe your habitat in detail in your *Activity Log*. Develop illustrations or make a scale model of the habitat and its surrounding environment.

GLOSSARY

Use the pronunciation key below to help you decode, or read, the pronunciations.

Pronunciation Key

a	at, bad	d	dear, soda, bad
ā	ape, pain, day, break	f	five, defend, leaf, off, cough, elephant
ä	father, car, heart	g	game, ago, fog, egg
âr	care, pair, bear, their, where	h	hat, ahead
e	end, pet, said, heaven, friend	hw	white, whether, which
ē	equal, me, feet, team, piece, key	j	joke, enjoy, gem, page, edge
i	it, big, English, hymn	k	kite, bakery, seek, tack, cat
ī	ice, fine, lie, my	l	lid, sailor, feel, ball, allow
îr	ear, deer, here, pierce	m	man, family, dream
o	odd, hot, watch	n	not, final, pan, knife
ō	old, oat, toe, low	ng	long, singer, pink
ô	coffee, all, taught, law, fought	p	pail, repair, soap, happy
ôr	order, fork, horse, story, pour	r	ride, parent, wear, more, marry
oi	oil, toy	s	sit, aside, pets, cent, pass
ou	out, now	sh	shoe, washer, fish mission, nation
u	up, mud, love, double	t	tag, pretend, fat, button, dressed
ū	use, mule, cue, feud, few	th	thin, panther, both
ü	rule, true, food	th	this, mother, smooth
ů	put, wood, should	v	very, favor, wave
ûr	burn, hurry, term, bird, word, courage	w	wet, weather, reward
ə	about, taken, pencil, lemon, circus	y	yes, onion
b	bat, above, job	z	zoo, lazy, jazz, rose, dogs, houses
ch	chin, such, match	zh	vision, treasure, seizure

abyssal plain (ə bis′ əl · plān) the flat bottom of the ocean that is covered with a layer of mud, sand, and remains of organisms that have drifted down for millions of years

autotrophic (ô tə tro′ pik) organisms, usually plants or bacteria, that produce food from inorganic (nonliving) substances

bathymetric maps (bath′ ə met′ rik) maps showing the depth of an area on the seafloor

beaches deposits of loose material that run parallel to the shoreline

benthos plants and animals that live on the ocean bottom

breakwater an artificial sandbar made of concrete or rock designed to weaken the effects of ocean waves

buoyancy (boi′ ən sē) the ability to control rising when submerged

buoyant (boi′ ənt) able to float or rise in water

chemosynthesis (kē′ mō sin′ thə sis) a process in which bacteria uses substances, such as methane gas, to produce food through chemical reactions

condensation (kon′ den sā′ shən) the change from the gaseous state to the liquid state

consumers (kən sü′ mərz) organisms that feed on producers

continental shelf (kon′ tə nen′ təl · shelf) the gently sloping underwater edge of a continent that extends from the shore to a depth of approximately 200 meters (600 feet)

continental slope (kon′ tə nen′ təl · slōp) the slope at the edge of the continental shelf that drops toward an abyssal plain

convection currents (kən vek′ shən · kûr′ ənts) currents driven by density differences

Coriolis effect the effect of Earth's rotation on the flow of currents

decomposers (dē′ kəm pō′ zərz) organisms that break down organic tissue into vital nutrients

desalination (dē sal′ ə nā′ shən) the removal of salts and other dissolved solids from water

downwelling (doun′ wel′ ing) the sinking of surface waters near a coast

ecosystems (ek′ ō sis′ təmz) complex systems of organisms interacting with each other in a physical and chemical environment

evaporation (i vap′ ə rā′ shən) a change from a liquid into a gas; vaporization

fetch (fech) the distance of open water over which wind blows

groins short walls built at right angles to the shore to trap moving sand

heterotrophic (het′ ər ə tro′ pik) organisms that are unable to make their own food to obtain energy

high tide a tide when the water is at its greatest elevation

infiltration (in fil′ trā′ shən) in the water cycle, the process of water seeping into Earth

jetties barriers that extend from the mouth of a river into the ocean

low tide a tide when the water is at its lowest decline

mid-ocean ridges (mid′ ō′ shən · rij əz) chains of mountains that run down the center of the ocean

nekton (nek′ ton) the group of marine animals that are able to control their location in the water by swimming

ocean current (ō′ shən · kûr′ ənt) a sustained movement of ocean water

plankton (plangk′ tən) tiny plant-like organisms called phytoplankton and animal-like organisms called zooplankton that float at or near the surface of the ocean

precipitation (pri sip′ i tā′ shən) any form of water that falls to Earth, such as rain, hail or snow

producers (prə dü′ sərz) organisms that synthesize or make food

rift valley a valley along the center of some mid-ocean ridges

runoff (run′ ôf′) rain or snow not absorbed by the soil, which forms surface streams

salinity (sə lin′ i tē) the saltiness of water

seawalls walls built along the shore as barriers to erosion

sonar (sō′ när) an instrument used to detect underwater objects and to determine their location by means of sound waves reflected from or produced by the objects

sublimation (sub′ lə mā′ shən) the direct change of state from a solid to a gas or a gas to a solid

surf breaking ocean waves

tide (tīd) the regular rise and fall of the ocean and bodies of water connected to it, caused by the gravitational pull of the moon and sun

transpiration (tran′ spə ra′ shən) the giving off of waste products in the form of vapor by a living organism, such as a plant

trenches (trench′ ez) long, narrow openings or deep furrows in the seafloor

tsunami (tsü nä′ mē) a large sea wave caused by sudden undersea movements like earthquakes

upwelling (up′ wel′ ing) the rising of colder, deeper waters to replace the water blown away

water cycle (wô′ tər · sī′ kəl) a large complex system in which water moves from place to place in different forms

INDEX

CREDITS

Photo Credits:

Cover, The Image Bank/Larry J. Pierce; **1,** E.R. Degginger; **3** (t) ©Studiohio (b) ©Herwarth Voightmann/Planet Earth Pictures; **5,** E.R. Degginger; **6, 7,** Art Wolfe/ALLSTOCK; **7, 9,** ©The Image Works; **10, 11,** ©Studiohio, (border) Fred Bavendam, ALLSTOCK; **12,** (tl) Dick Durrance III/The Stock Market, (bl) Ron Thomas/FPG International; **12, 13,** Myrleen Ferguson/Photoedit; **14,** (l) ©Comstock Inc., (r) Bob Barbour/ALLSTOCK; **15,** (tr) ©Richard H. Gross/Biological Photography, (bl) ©John Lythgoe/Planet Earth Pictures, (br) ©Richard Coomber/Planet Earth Pictures; **16, 17,** ©Studiohio; **20,** E.R. Degginger; **21,** ©Aaron Haupt; **24,** ©Pete Atkins/Planet Earth Pictures; **25,** ©John Lythgoe/Planet Earth Pictures; **26,** ©John Downer/Planet Earth Pictures; **27,** (t) Galen Rowell/Mountain Light, (l) ©John Lythgoe/Planet Earth Pictures, (r) Tom Bean/ALLSTOCK, (b) Frans Lanting/ALLSTOCK; **28,** Shooting Star; **30,** ©Mike Moir, (bl) © Dave Lyons/Planet Earth Pictures; **32, 33,** ©Studiohio; **35,** (l) © Fred Ward/Black Star, (r) ©Flip Schulke/Planet Earth Pictures; **37,** ©Manfred Kage/Peter Arnold, Inc.; **43,** World Ocean Floor/Bruce Heezen & Marie Tharp; **44,** Woods Hole Oceanographic Institution/ Quest Group Ltd.; **46, 47,** J. Boeder/ALLSTOCK; **50, 51,** ©Studiohio; **53,** Univ. of Miami Rosenstiel School of Marine and Atmospheric Science; **57, 60,** E.R. Degginger; **61,** (t) Phil Degginger, (b) ©Brent Turner/BLT Productions/1991; **63,** L.J. Tinstman/Profiles West; **66, 67,** E.R. Degginger; **68,** Stephen Frink/ALLSTOCK; **69,** ©Herwarth Voigtmann/Planet Earth Pictures; **70,** E.R. Degginger; **71,** (l) (tr) E.R. Degginger, (br) Welzenbach/The Stock Market; **75,** ©Robert Hessler/Planet Earth Pictures; **77,** ©Peter David/Planet Earth Pictures; **78,** (tl) ©Marty Snyderman/Planet Earth Pictures, (tr) ©Georgette Douwma/Planet Earth Pictures, (bl) ©Peter Scoones/Planet Earth Pictures, (bm) (br) ©A. Kerstitch/Planet Earth Pictures; **79,** Field Museum of Natural History; **80,** ©Kurt Amsler/Planet Earth Pictures; **81,** ©Dann Blackwood; **82,** ©Manfred P. Kage/Peter Arnold, Inc.; **84, 85,** Ron Sanford/ALLSTOCK; **86, 87,** ©Studiohio; **88,** (t) ©Porterfield-Chickering/Photo Researchers, (bl) Suzanne Brookens/The Stock Market, (br) ©Ty & Julie Hotchkiss/Photo Researchers; **88, 89,** (border) ©Comstock, Inc.; **89,** (t) ©Lowell Georgia/Photo Researchers, (b) ©John Menzies/Planet Earth Pictures; **90,** ©Georgette Douwma/Planet Earth Pictures; **90, 91,** (border) ©Georgette Douwma/Planet Earth Pictures; **91,** Ken Straiton/The Stock Market; **92,** Robert Young Pelton/Westlight; **93,** ©Richard H. Gross/Biological Photography; **94,** Robert Holland Photography; **95,** (tl) (b) ©Robert Holland Photography, (tr) ©Fred Ward/Black Star; **96,** Jon Lamar/The Stock Market; **97,** (t) ©Chris Howes/Planet Earth Pictures, (b) John Scheiber/The Stock Market; **98,** ©Mike Potts/Planet Earth Pictures; **100,** (t) (m) Dr. Christopher Clark/Cornell Laboratory of Ornithology Bioacoustics Research Program, (b) Mary Lou Jones & Steven L. Swartz, Ph.D.; **101,** ©Duncan Murrell/Planet Earth Pictures; **102,** Bill Roth/Gamma Liaison; **103,** L. Cottrell/Gamma Liaison; **104,** (tl) L. Cottrell/Gamma Liaison, (tr) Bill Roth/Gamma Liaison.

Illustration Credits:

7, 15, 29, 65, 83, 99, James Shough; **14, 15, 48, 49, 52, 54,** David Reed; **18, 19, 56, 57,** Ebet Dudley; **21,** Howard Friedman; **22, 55, 59,** Thomas Kennedy; **28, 38, 62, 63,** John Edwards; **37, 40, 41,** Bill Boyer; **36,** JAK Graphics; **39, 58, 59, 72, 76, 77, 105,** Greg Harris